权威中英双语插图典藏版

飞鸟集·新月集

Stray Birds &
The Crescent Moon

[印]罗宾德拉纳特·泰戈尔 （Tagore Rabindranath） ◎著

郑振铎◎译

湖南文艺出版社
HUNAN LITERATURE AND ART PUBLISHING HOUSE

图书在版编目（CIP）数据

飞鸟集·新月集：汉英对照 /（印）泰戈尔（Tagore,R.）著；
郑振铎译. —长沙：湖南文艺出版社，2011.1
书名原文：Stray Birds&The Crescent Moon
ISBN 978-7-5404-4724-3

Ⅰ.①飞… Ⅱ.①泰… ②郑… Ⅲ.①英语—汉语—对照读物
②诗歌—作品集—印度—现代③散文诗—作品集—印度—现代
Ⅳ.① H319.4：I

中国版本图书馆 CIP 数据核字 (2010) 第 243444 号

上架建议：青少年阅读·经典名著

飞鸟集·新月集

作　　者：[印]罗宾德拉纳特·泰戈尔（Tagore Rabindranath）
译　　者：郑振铎
出 版 人：刘清华
责任编辑：徐小芳
整体监制：吴成玮
策划编辑：薛　婷
版式设计：风　筝
封面设计：张丽娜
出版发行：湖南文艺出版社
　　　　　（长沙市雨花区东二环一段 508 号　邮编：410014）
网　　址：www.hnwy.net
印　　刷：北京天宇万达印刷有限公司
经　　销：新华书店
开　　本：880×1230　1/32
字　　数：100 千字
印　　张：9
版　　次：2011 年 1 月第 1 版
印　　次：2017 年 1 月第 10 次印刷
书　　号：ISBN 978-7-5404-4724-3
定　　价：22.00 元

质量监督电话：010-59096394
团购电话：010-59320018

目录
CONTENTS

目录
CONTENTS

飞鸟集

使生如夏花之绚烂，死如秋叶之静美。

一九二二年版《飞鸟集》例言

译诗是一件最不容易的工作。原诗音节的保留固然是绝不可能的事！就是原诗意义的完全移植，也有十分的困难。散文诗算是最容易译的，但有时也须费十分的力气。如惠德曼[1]（Walt Whitman）的《草叶集》便是一个例子。这有二个原因：第一，有许多诗中特用的美丽文句，差不多是不能移动的。在一种文字里，这种字眼是"诗的"是"美的"，如果把它移植在第二种文字中，不是找不到相当的好字，便是把原意丑化了，变成非"诗的"了。在泰戈尔的《人格论》中，曾讨论到这一层。他以为诗总是要选择那"有生气的"字眼——就是那些不仅仅为报告用而能融化于我们心中，不因市井常用而损坏它的形式的字眼。譬如在英文里，"意识"（consciousness）这个字，带有多少

---

[1] 即惠特曼。——编者注

科学的意义，所以诗中不常用它。印度文的同意字 chetana 则是一个"有生气"而常用于诗歌里的字。又如英文的"感情"（feeling）这个字是充满了生命的，但彭加利文 ① 里的同义字 anubhuti 则诗中绝无用之者。在这些地方，译诗的人实在感到万分的困难。第二，诗歌的文句总是含蓄的，暗示的。他的句法的构造，多简短而含义丰富。有的时候，简直不能译。如直译，则不能达意。如稍加诠释，则又把原文的风韵与含蓄完全消灭，而使之不成一首诗了。

因此，我主张诗集的介绍，只应当在可能的范围选择，而不能——也不必——完全整册地搬运过来。

大概诗歌的选译，有两个方便的地方：第一，选择可以适应译者的兴趣。在一个诗集中的许多诗，译者未必都十分喜欢它。如果不十分喜欢他，不十分感觉得它的美好，则他的译文必不能十分得神，至少也把这快乐的工作变成一种无意义的苦役。选译则可以减灭译者的这层痛苦。第二，便是减少上述的两层翻译上的困难。因为如此便可以把不能译的诗，不必译出来。译出来而丑化了或是为读者所看不懂，则反不如不译的好。

但我并不是在这里宣传选译主义。诗集的全选，是我所极端希望而且欢迎的。不过这种工作应当让给那些有全译能力的译者去做。我为自己的兴趣与能力所限制，实在不敢担任这种重大的工作。且为大多数的译者计，我也主张选译是较好的一种译诗方法。

现在我译泰戈尔的诗，便实行了这种选译的主张，以前我也有全

---

① 即孟加拉文。——编者注

译泰戈尔各诗集的野心。有好些友人也极力劝我把它们全译出来。我试了几次。但我的野心与被大家鼓起的勇气，终于给我的能力与兴趣打败了。

现在所译的泰戈尔各集的诗，都是我所最喜欢读的，而且是我的能力所比较的能够译得出的。

有许多诗，我自信是能够译得出的，但因为自己翻译它们的兴趣不大强烈，便不高兴去译它们。还有许多诗我是很喜欢读它们，而且是极愿意把它们译出来的，但因为自己能力的不允许，便也只好舍弃了它们。

即在这些译出的诗中，有许多也是自己觉得译得不好，心中很不满意的。但实在不忍再割舍它们了。只好请读者赏读它的原意，不必注意于粗陋的译文。

泰戈尔的诗集用英文出版的共有六部：

（一）《园丁集》（Gardener）

（二）《吉檀迦利》（Jitanjali）

（三）《新月集》（Crescent Moon）

（四）《采果集》（Fruit-Gathering）

（五）《飞鸟集》（Stray Birds）

（六）《爱者之贻与歧路》（Lover's Gift And Crossing）

但据 B. K. Roy 的《泰戈尔与其诗》（R. Tagore：The Man And His Poetry）一书上所载，他用彭加利文写的重要诗集，却有下面的许多种：

Sandhva Sangit, Kshanika,

Probhat Sangit，Kanika，

Bhanusingher Padabali，Kahini，

Chabi O Gan，Sishn，

Kari O Komal，Naibadya，

Prakritir Pratisodh，Utsharga，

Sonartari，Kheya，

Chaitali，Gitanzali，

Kalpana，Gitimal ya，

Katha.

我的这几本诗选，是根据那六部用英文写的诗集译下来的。因为我不懂梵文。

在这几部诗集中，间有重出的诗篇，如《海边》一诗，已见于《新月集》中，而又列入《吉檀迦利》，排为第六十首。《飞鸟集》的第九十八首，也与同集中的第二百六十三首相同。像这一类的诗篇，都照先见之例，把它列入最初见的地方。①

我的译文自信是很忠实的。误解的地方，却也保不定完全没有。如读者偶有发现，肯公开地指教我，那是我所异常欢迎的。

郑振铎　一九二二，六，二六。

---

① 参照人民文学出版社一九六一年版《泰戈尔作品集》,《海边》一诗未列入《新月集》而归入《吉檀迦利》。集中其他重复之诗章，亦以上述作品集为准排列。——编者

一九三三年版本序

《飞鸟集》曾经全译出来一次，因为我自己的不满意，所以又把它删节为现在的选译本 ①。以前，我曾看见有人把这诗集选译过，但似乎错得太多，因此我译时不曾拿它来参考。

近来小诗十分发达。它们的作者大半都是直接或间接受泰戈尔此集的影响的。此集的介绍，对于没有机会得读原文的，至少总有些贡献。

这诗集的一部分译稿是积了许多时候的，但大部分却都是在西湖俞楼译的。

我在此谢谢叶圣陶、徐玉诺二君。他们替我很仔细地校读过这部译文，并且供给了许多重要的意见给我。

郑振铎　六,二六。

---

① 本书的《飞鸟集》，是增补完备的全译本。——编者注

001

Stray birds of summer come to my window to sing and fly away. And yellow leaves of autumn, which have no songs, flutter and fall there with a sigh.

夏天的飞鸟，飞到我窗前唱歌，又飞去了。

秋天的黄叶，它们没有什么可唱，只叹息一声，飞落在那里。

002

O troupe of little vagrants of the world, leave your footprints in my words.

世界上的一队小小的漂泊者呀，请留下你们的足印在我的文字里。

003

The world puts off its mask of vastness to its lover. It becomes small as one song, as one kiss of the eternal.

世界对着它的爱人，把它浩瀚的面具揭下了。

它变小了，小如一首歌，小如一回永恒的接吻。

004

It is the tears of the earth that keep her smiles in bloom.

是大地的泪点，使她的微笑保持着青春不谢。

005

The mighty desert is burning for the love of a blade of grass who shakes her head and laughs and flies away.

无垠的沙漠热烈追求一叶绿草的爱，她摇摇头笑着飞开了。

006

If you shed tears when you miss the sun, you also miss the stars.

如果你因失去了太阳而流泪，那么你也将失去群星了。

007

The sands in your way beg for your song and your movement, dancing water. Will you carry the burden of their lameness?

跳舞着的流水呀，在你途中的泥沙，要求你的歌声，你的流动呢。你肯挟跛足的泥沙而俱下么?

008

Her wistful face haunts my dreams like the rain at night.

她的热切的脸，如夜雨似的，搅扰着我的梦魂。

009

Once we dreamt that we were strangers. We wake up to find that we were dear to each other.

有一次，我们梦见大家都是不相识的。

我们醒了，却知道我们原是相亲相爱的。

010

Sorrow is hushed into peace in my heart like the evening among the silent trees.

忧思在我的心里平静下去，正如暮色降临在寂静的山林中。

011

Some unseen fingers, like an idle breeze, are playing upon my heart the music of the ripples.

有些看不见的手指，如懒懒的微飔似的，正在我的心上奏着潺潺的乐声。

012

"What language is thine, O sea?"

"The language of eternal question."

"What language is thy answer, O sky?"

"The language of eternal silence."

"海水呀，你说的是什么？"

"是永恒的疑问。"

"天空呀，你回答的话是什么？"

"是永恒的沉默。"

013

Listen, my heart, to the whispers of the world with which it makes love to you.

静静地听，我的心呀，听那世界的低语，这是它对你求爱的表示呀。

014

The mystery of creation is like the darkness of night—it is great. Delusions of knowledge are like the fog of the morning.

创造的神秘，有如夜间的黑暗——是伟大的。而知识的幻影却不过如晨间之雾。

015

Do not seat your love upon a precipice because it is high.

不要因为峭壁是高的，便让你的爱情坐在峭壁上。

016

I sit at my window this morning where the world like a passer—by stops for a moment, nods to me and goes.

我今晨坐在窗前，世界如一个过路人似的，停留了一会，向我点点头又走过去了。

017

These little thoughts are the rustle of leaves; they have their whisper of joy in my mind.

这些微思，是绿叶的簌簌之声呀；它们在我的心里欢悦地微语着。

018

What you are you do not see, what you see is your shadow.

你看不见你自己，你所看见的只是你的影子。

019

My wishes are fools, they shout across thy songs, my Master. Let me but listen.

神呀，我的那些愿望真是愚傻呀，它们杂在你的歌声中喧叫着呢。让我只是静听着吧。

020

I cannot choose the best. The best chooses me.

我不能选择那最好的。
是那最好的选择我。

021

They throw their shadows before them who carry their
lantern on their back.

那些把灯背在背上的人，把他们的影子投到了自己前面。

022

That I exist is a perpetual surprise which is life.

我的存在，对我是一个永久的神奇，这就是生活。

023

"We, the rustling leaves, have a voice that answers the storms, but who are you so silent?"

"I am a mere flower."

"我们萧萧的树叶都有声响回答那风和雨。你是谁呢，那样的沉默着？"

"我不过是一朵花。"

024

Rest belongs to the work as the eyelids to the eyes.

休息与工作的关系，正如眼睑与眼睛的关系。

025

Man is a born child, his power is the power of growth.

人是一个初生的孩子，他的力量，就是生长的力量。

026

God expects answers for the flowers he sends us, not for the sun and the earth.

神希望我们酬答他，在于他送给我们的花朵，而不在于太阳和土地。

027

The light that plays, like a naked child, among the green leaves happily knows not that man can lie.

光明如一个裸体的孩子，快快活活地在绿叶当中游戏，它不知道人是会欺诈的。

028

O Beauty, find thyself in love, not in the flattery of thy mirror.

啊，美呀，在爱中找你自己吧，不要到你镜子的谄谀中去找寻。

029

My heart beats her waves at the shore of the world and writes upon it her signature in tears with the words, "I love thee."

我的心把她的波浪在世界的海岸上冲激着，以热泪在上边写着她的题记："我爱你。"

030

"Moon, for what do you wait?"
"To salute the sun for whom I must make way."

"月儿呀，你在等候什么呢？"
"向我将让位给他的太阳致敬。"

031

The trees come up to my window like the yearning voice of the dumb earth.

绿树长到了我的窗前，仿佛是喑哑的大地发出的渴望的声音。

032

His own mornings are new surprises to God.

神自己的清晨，在他自己看来也是新奇的。

033

Life finds its wealth by the claims of the world, and its worth by the claims of love.

生命从世界得到资产，爱情使它得到价值。

034

The dry river—bed finds no thanks for its past.

枯竭的河床，并不感谢它的过去。

035

The bird wishes it were a cloud. The cloud wishes it were a bird.

鸟儿愿为一朵云。

云儿愿为一只鸟。

036

The waterfall sings, "I find my song, when I find my freedom."

瀑布歌唱道："我得到自由时便有歌声了。"

037

I cannot tell why this heart languishes in silence. It is for small needs it never asks, or knows or remembers.

我说不出这心为什么那样默默地颓丧着。

是为了它那不曾要求、不曾知道、不曾记得的小小的需要。

038

Woman, when you move about in your household service your limbs sing like a hill stream among its pebbles.

妇人，你在料理家事的时候，你的手足歌唱着，正如山间的溪水歌唱着在小石中流过。

039

The sun goes to cross the Western sea, leaving its last salutation to the East.

当太阳横过西方的海面时，对着东方留下他最后的敬礼。

040

Do not blame your food because you have no appetite.

不要因为你自己没有胃口而去责备你的食物。

041

The trees, like the longings of the earth, stand a-tiptoe to peep at the heaven.

群树如表示大地的愿望似的，踮起脚来向天空窥望。

042

You smiled and talked to me of nothing and I felt that for this I had been waiting long.

你微微地笑着，不同我说什么话。而我觉得，为了这个，我已等待得久了。

043

The fish in the water is silent, the animal on the earth is noisy, the bird in the air is singing. But Man has in him the silence of the sea, the noise of the earth and the music of the air.

水里的游鱼是沉默的。陆地上的兽类是喧闹的，空中的飞鸟是歌唱着的。

但是，人类却兼有海里的沉默、地上的喧闹与空中的音乐。

044

The world rushes on over the strings of the lingering heart making the music of sadness.

世界在踌躇之心的琴弦上跑过去，奏出忧郁的乐声。

045

He has made his weapons his gods. When his weapons win he is defeated himself.

他把他的刀剑当做他的上帝。
当他的刀剑胜利时他自己却失败了。

046

God finds himself by creating.

神从创造中找到他自己。

047

Shadow, with her veil drawn, follows Light in secret meekness, with her silent steps of love.

阴影戴上她的面幕，秘密地，温顺地，用她的沉默的爱的脚步，跟在"光"后边。

048

The stars are not afraid to appear like fireflies.

群星不怕显得像萤火那样。

049

I thank thee that I am none of the wheels of power but I am one with the living creatures that are crushed by it.

谢谢神，我不是一个权力的轮子，而是被压在这轮下的活人之一。

050

The mind, sharp but not broad, sticks at every point but does not move.

心是尖锐的，不是宽博的，它执著在每一点上，却并不活动。

051

Your idol is shattered in the dust to prove that God's dust is greater than your idol.

你的偶像委散在尘土中了，这可证明神的尘土比你的偶像还伟大。

052

Man does not reveal himself in his history, he struggles up through it.

人不能在他的历史中表现出他自己，他在历史中奋斗着露出头角。

053

While the glass lamp rebukes the earthen for calling it cousin, the moon rises, and the glass lamp, with a bland smile, calls her, "My dear, dear sister."

玻璃灯因为瓦灯叫它做表兄而责备瓦灯。但当明月出来时，玻璃灯却温和地微笑着，叫明月为——"我亲爱的，亲爱的姐姐。"

054

Like the meeting of the seagulls and the waves we meet and come near. The seagulls fly off, the waves roll away and we depart.

我们如海鸥之与波涛相遇似的，遇见了，走近了。海鸥飞去，波涛滚滚地流开，我们也分别了。

055

My day is done, and I am like a boat drawn on the beach, listening to the dance-music of the tide in the evening.

我的白昼已经完了，我像一只泊在海滩上的小船，谛听着晚潮跳舞的乐声。

056

Life is given to us, we earn it by giving it.

我们的生命是天赋的，我们唯有献出生命，才能得到生命。

057

We come nearest to the great when we are great in humility.

当我们是大为谦卑的时候，便是我们最近于伟大的时候。

058

The sparrow is sorry for the peacock at the burden of its tail.

麻雀看见孔雀负担着它的翎尾，替它担忧。

059

Never be afraid of the moments—thus sings the voice of the everlasting.

决不要害怕刹那——永恒之声这样唱着。

060

The hurricane seeks the shortest road by the no-road, and suddenly ends its search in the Nowhere.

飓风于无路之中寻求最短之路，又突然地在"无何有之国"终止了它的寻求。

061

Take my wine in my own cup, friend. It loses its wreath of foam when poured into that of others.

在我自己的杯中，饮了我的酒吧，朋友。

一倒在别人的杯里，这酒的腾跳的泡沫便要消失了。

062

The Perfect decks itself in beauty for the love of the Imperfect.

"完全"为了对"不全"的爱，把自己装饰得美丽。

063

God says to man, "I heal you therefore I hurt, love you therefore punish."

神对人说道："我医治你所以伤害你，爱你所以惩罚你。"

064

Thank the flame for its light, but do not forget the lampholder standing in the shade with constancy of patience.

谢谢火焰给你光明，但是不要忘了那执灯的人，他是坚忍地站在黑暗当中呢。

065

Tiny grass, your steps are small, but you possess the earth under your tread.

小草呀，你的足步虽小，但是你拥有你足下的土地。

066

The infant flower opens its bud and cries, "Dear World, please do not fade."

幼花的蓓蕾开放了，它叫道："亲爱的世界呀，请不要萎谢了。"

067

God grows weary of great kingdoms, but never of little flowers.

神对于那些大帝国会感到厌恶，却决不会厌恶那些小小的花朵。

068

Wrong cannot afford defeat but Right can.

错误经不起失败，但是真理却不怕失败。

069

"I give my whole water in joy," sings the waterfall, "though little of it is enough for the thirsty."

瀑布歌唱道："虽然渴者只要少许的水便够了，我却很快活地给予了我全部的水。"

070

Where is the fountain that throws up these flowers in a ceaseless outbreak of ecstasy?

把那些花朵抛掷上去的那一阵子无休无止的狂欢大喜的劲儿，其源泉是在哪里呢？

071

The woodcutter's axe begged for its handle from the tree. The tree gave it.

樵夫的斧头，问树要斧柄。

树便给了他。

072

In my solitude of heart I feel the sigh of this widowed evening veiled with mist and rain.

这寡独的黄昏，幕着雾与雨，我在我心的孤寂里，感觉到它的叹息。

073

Chastity is a wealth that comes from abundance of love.

贞操是从丰富的爱情中生出来的财富。

074

The mist, like love, plays upon the heart of the hills and brings out surprises of beauty.

雾，像爱情一样，在山峰的心上游戏，生出种种美丽的变幻。

075

We read the world wrong and say that it deceives us.

我们把世界看错了，反说它欺骗我们。

076

The poet wind is out over the sea and the forest to seek his own voice.

诗人——飙风，正出经海洋和森林，追求它自己的歌声。

077

Every child comes with the message that God is not yet discouraged of man.

每一个孩子出生时都带来信息说：神对人并未灰心失望。

078

The grass seeks her crowd in the earth. The tree seeks his solitude of the sky.

绿草求她地上的伴侣。
树木求他天空的寂寞。

079

Man barricades against himself.

人对他自己建筑起堤防来。

080

Your voice, my friend, wanders in my heart, like the muffled sound of the sea among these listening pines.

我的朋友，你的语声飘荡在我的心里，像那海水的低吟声缭绕在静听着的松林之间。

081

What is this unseen flame of darkness whose sparks are the stars?

这个不可见的黑暗之火焰，以繁星为其火花的，到底是什么呢？

082

Let life be beautiful like summer flowers and death like autumn leaves.

使生如夏花之绚烂，死如秋叶之静美。

083

He who wants to do good knocks at the gate; he who loves finds the gate open.

那想做好人的，在门外敲着门；那爱人的，看见门敞开着。

084

In death the many becomes one; in life the one becomes many. Religion will be one when God is dead.

在死的时候，众多合而为一；在生的时候，一化为众多。
神死了的时候，宗教便将合而为一。

085

The artist is the lover of Nature, therefore he is her slave and her master.

艺术家是自然的情人，所以他是自然的奴隶，也是自然的主人。

086

"How far are you from me, O Fruit?"
"I am hidden in your heart, O Flower."

"你离我有多远呢,果实呀?"
"我藏在你心里呢,花呀。"

087

This longing is for the one who is felt in the dark, but not seen in the day.

这个渴望是为了那个在黑夜里感觉得到、在大白天里却看不见的人。

088

"You are the big drop of dew under the lotus leaf, I am the smaller one on its upper side," said the dew drop to the lake.

露珠对湖水说道:"你是在荷叶下面的大露珠,我是在荷叶上面的较小的露珠。"

089

The scabbard is content to be dull when it protects the keenness of the sword.

刀鞘保护刀的锋利，它自己则满足于它的迟钝。

090

In darkness the One appears as uniform; in the light the One appears as manifold.

在黑暗中，"一"视若一体；在光亮中，"一"便视若众多。

091

The great earth makes herself hospitable with the help of the grass.

大地借助于绿草，显出她自己的殷勤好客。

092

The birth and death of the leaves are the rapid whirls of the eddy whose wider circles move slowly among stars.

绿叶的生与死乃是旋风的急骤的旋转，它的更广大的旋转的圈子乃是在天上繁星之间徐缓的转动。

093

Power said to the world, "Your are mine." The world kept it prisoner on her throne. Love said to the world, "I am thine." The world gave it the freedom of her house.

权势对世界说道："你是我的。"

世界便把权势囚禁在她的宝座下面。

爱情对世界说道："我是你的。"

世界便给予爱情以在她屋内来往的自由。

094

The mist is like the earth's desire. It hides the sun for whom
she cries.

浓雾仿佛是大地的愿望。

它藏起了太阳，而太阳原是她所呼求的。

095

Be still, my heart, these great trees are prayers.

安静些吧，我的心，这些大树都是祈祷者呀。

096

The noise of the moment scoffs at the music of the Eternal.

瞬刻的喧声，讥笑着永恒的音乐。

097

I think of other ages that floated upon the stream of life and love and death and are forgotten, and I feel the freedom of passing, away.

我想起了浮泛在生与爱与死的川流上的许多别的时代，以及这些时代之被遗忘，我便感觉到离开尘世的自由了。

098

The sadness of my soul is her bride's veil. It waits to be lifted in the night.

我灵魂里的忧郁就是她的新婚的面纱。

这面纱等候着在夜间卸去。

099

Death's stamp gives value to the coin of life; making it possible to buy with life what is truly precious.

死之印记给生的钱币以价值，使它能够用生命来购买那真正的宝物。

100

The cloud stood humbly in a corner of the sky. The morning crowned it with splendor.

白云谦逊地站在天之一隅。

晨光给它戴上了霞彩。

101

The dust receives insult and in return offers her flowers.

尘土受到损辱，却以她的花朵来报答。

102

Do not linger to gather flowers to keep them, but walk on, for flowers will keep themselves blooming all your way.

只管走过去，不必逗留着采了花朵来保存，因为一路上花朵自会继续开放的。

103

Roots are the branches down in the earth. Branches are roots in the air.

根是地下的枝。
枝是空中的根。

104

The music of the far-away summer flutters around the autumn seeking its former nest.

远远去了的夏之音乐，翱翔于秋间，寻求它的旧垒。

105

Do not insult your friend by lending him merits from your own pocket.

不要从你自己的袋里掏出勋绩借给你的朋友，这是污辱他的。

106

The touch of the nameless days clings to my heart like mosses round the old tree.

无名的日子的感触，攀缘在我的心上，正像那绿色的苔藓，攀缘在老树的周身。

107

The echo mocks her origin to prove she is the original.

回声嘲笑着她的原声，以证明她是原声。

108

God is ashamed when the prosperous boasts of his special favor.

当富贵利达的人夸说他得到神的特别恩惠时，上帝却羞了。

109

I cast my own shadow upon my path, because I have a lamp that has not been lighted.

我投射我自己的影子在我的路上，因为我有一盏还没有燃点起来的明灯。

110

Man goes into the noisy crowd to drown his own clamor of silence.

人走进喧哗的群众里去，为的是要淹没他自己的沉默的呼号。

111

That which ends in exhaustion is death, but the perfect ending is in the endless.

终止于衰竭的是"死亡"，但"圆满"却终止于无穷。

112

The sun has his simple robe of light. The clouds are decked with gorgeousness.

太阳只穿一件朴素的光衣，白云却披了灿烂的裙裾。

113

The hills are like shouts of children who raise their arms, trying to catch stars.

山峰如群儿之喧嚷，举起他们的双臂，想去捉天上的星星。

114

The road is lonely in its crowd for it is not loved.

道路虽然拥挤，却是寂寞的，因为它是不被爱的。

115

The power that boasts of its mischiefs is laughed at by the yellow leaves that fall, and clouds that pass by.

权势以它的恶行自夸，落下的黄叶与浮游的云片却在笑它。

116

The earth hums to me today in the sun, like a woman at her spinning, some ballad of the ancient time in a forgotten tongue.

今天大地在太阳光里向我营营哼鸣，像一个织着布的妇人，用一种已经被忘却的语言，哼着一些古代的歌曲。

117

The grass—blade is worthy of the great world where it grows.

绿草是无愧于它所生长的伟大世界的。

118

Dream is a wife who must talk. Sleep is a husband who silently suffers.

梦是一个一定要谈话的妻子，
睡眠是一个默默地忍受的丈夫。

119

The night kisses the fading day whispering to his ear, "I am death, your mother. I am to give you fresh birth."

夜与逝去的日子接吻，轻轻地在他耳旁说道："我是死，是你的母亲。我就要给你以新的生命。"

120

I feel thy beauty, dark night, like that of the loved woman when she has put out the lamp.

黑夜呀，我感觉到你的美了。你的美如一个可爱的妇人，当她把灯灭了的时候。

121

I carry in my world that flourishes the worlds that have failed.

我把在那些已逝去的世界上的繁荣带到我的世界上来。

122

Dear friend, I feel the silence of your great thoughts of many a deepening eventide on this beach when I listen to these waves.

亲爱的朋友呀，当我静听着海涛时，我好几次在暮色深沉的黄昏里，在这个海岸上，感到你的伟大思想的沉默了。

123

The bird thinks it is an act of kindness to give the fish a lift in the air.

鸟以为把鱼举在空中是一种慈善的举动。

124

"In the moon thou sendest thy love letters to me," said the night to the sun.

"I leave my answers in tears upon the grass."

夜对太阳说道："在月亮中，你送了你的情书给我。"

"我已在绿草上留下我的流着泪点的回答了。"

125

The Great is a born child; when he dies he gives his great childhood to the world.

伟人是一个天生的孩子，当他死时，他把他的伟大的孩提时代给了世界。

126

Not hammer-strokes, but dance of the water sings the pebbles into perfection.

不是槌的打击，乃是水的载歌载舞，使鹅卵石臻于完美。

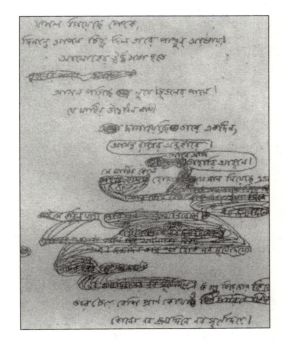

127

Bees sip honey from flowers and hum their thanks when they leave. The gaudy butterfly is sure that the flowers owe thanks to him.

蜜蜂从花中啜蜜，离开时营营地道谢。
浮华的蝴蝶却相信花是应该向它道谢的。

128

To be outspoken is easy when you do not wait to speak the complete truth.

如果你不等待着要说出完全的真理，那么把真话说出来是很容易的。

129

Asks the Possible to the Impossible, "Where is your dwelling-place?"
"In the dreams of the impotent," comes the answer.

"可能"问"不可能"道：
"你住在什么地方呢？"
它回答道："在那无能为力者的梦境里。"

130

If you shut your door to all errors truth will be shut out.

如果你把所有的错误都关在门外时，真理也要被关在外面了。

131

I hear some rustle of things behind my sadness of heart—I cannot see them.

我听见有些东西在我心的忧闷后面萧萧作响——我不能看见它们。

132

Leisure in its activity is work. The stillness of the sea stirs in waves.

闲暇在动作时便是工作。
静止的海水荡动时便成波涛。

133

The leaf becomes flower when it loves. The flower becomes fruit when it worships.

绿叶恋爱时便成了花。

花崇拜时便成了果实。

134

The roots below the earth claim no rewards for making the branches fruitful.

埋在地下的树根使树枝产生果实，却不要求什么报酬。

135

This rainy evening the wind is restless. I look at the swaying branches and ponder over the greatness of all things.

阴雨的黄昏，风无休止地吹着。

我看着摇曳的树枝，想念着万物的伟大。

136

Storm of midnight, like a giant child awakened in the untimely dark, has begun to play and shout.

子夜的风雨，如一个巨大的孩子，在不合时宜的黑夜里醒来，开始游戏和喧闹。

137

Thou raisest thy waves vainly to follow thy lover, O sea, thou lonely bride of the storm.

海呀，你这暴风雨的孤寂的新妇呀，你虽掀起波浪追随你的情人，但是无用呀。

138

"I am ashamed of my emptiness," said the Word to the Work.

"I know how poor I am when I see you," said the Work to the Word.

文字对工作说道："我惭愧我的空虚。"

工作对文字说道："当我看见你时，我便知道我是怎样地贫乏了。"

139

Time is the wealth of change, but the clock in its parody makes it mere change and no wealth.

时间是变化的财富。时钟模仿它，却只有变化而无财富。

140

Truth in her dress finds facts too tight. In fiction she moves with ease.

真理穿了衣裳，觉得事实太拘束了。

在想象中，她却转动得很舒畅。

141

When I traveled to here and to there, I was tired of thee, O Road, but now when thou leadest me to everywhere I am wedded to thee in love.

当我到这里那里旅行着时，路呀，我厌倦你了；但是现在，当你引导我到各处去时，我便爱上你，与你结婚了。

142

Let me think that there is one among those stars that guides my life through the dark unknown.

让我设想，在群星之中，有一颗星是指导着我的生命通过不可知的黑暗的。

143

Woman, with the grace of your fingers you touched my things and order came out like music.

妇人，你用了你美丽的手指，触着我的什物，秩序便如音乐似的生出来了。

144

One sad voice has its nest among the ruins of the years. It sings to me in the night, — "I loved you."

一个忧郁的声音，筑巢于逝水似的年华中。

它在夜里向我唱道："我爱你。"

145

The flaming fire warns me off by its own glow. Save me from the dying embers hidden under ashes.

燃着的火，以它熊熊的光焰警告我不要走近它。

把我从潜藏在灰中的余烬里救出来吧。

146

I have my stars in the sky, but oh for my little lamp unlit in my house.

我有群星在天上，

但是，唉，我屋里的小灯却没有点亮。

147

The dust of the dead words clings to thee. Wash thy soul with silence.

死文字的尘土沾着你。

用沉默去洗净你的灵魂吧。

148

Gaps are left in life through which comes the sad music of death.

生命里留了许多罅隙，从中送来了死之忧郁的音乐。

149

The world has opened its heart of light in the morning. Come out, my heart, with thy love to meet it.

世界已在早晨敞开了它的光明之心。

出来吧，我的心，带着你的爱去与它相会。

150

My thoughts shimmer with these shimmering leaves and my heart sings with the touch of this sunlight; my life is glad to be floating with all things into the blue of space, into the dark of time.

我的思想随着这些闪耀的绿叶而闪耀；我的心灵因了这日光的抚触而歌唱；我的生命因为偕了万物一同浮泛在空间的蔚蓝、时间的墨黑中而感到欢快。

151

God's great power is in the gentle breeze, not in the storm.

神的巨大的威权是在柔和的微飔里，而不在狂风暴雨之中。

152

This is a dream in which things are all loose and they oppress.
I shall find them gathered in thee when I awake and shall be free.

在梦中，一切事都散漫着，都压着我，但这不过是一个梦呀。当
我醒来时，我便将觉得这些事都已聚集在你那里，我也便将自由了。

153

"Who is there to take up my duties?" asked the setting sun.
"I shall do what I can, my Master," said the earthen lamp.

落日问道："有谁继续我的职务呢？"
瓦灯说道："我要尽我所能地做去，我的主人。"

154

By plucking her petals you do not gather the beauty of the flower.

采着花瓣时，得不到花的美丽。

155

Silence will carry your voice like the nest that holds the sleeping birds.

沉默蕴蓄着语声，正如鸟巢拥围着睡鸟。

156

The Great walks with the Small without fear.
The Middling keeps aloof.

大的不怕与小的同游。
居中的却远而避之。

157

The night opens the flowers in secret and allows the day to get thanks.

夜秘密地把花开放了，却让那白日去领受谢词。

158

Power takes as ingratitude the writhings of its victims.

权势认为牺牲者的痛苦是忘恩负义。

159

When we rejoice in our fullness, then we can part with our fruits with joy.

当我们以我们的充实为乐时，那么，我们便能很快乐地跟我们的果实分手了。

160

The raindrops kissed the earth and whispered,— "We are thy homesick children, mother, come back to thee from the heaven."

雨点吻着大地，微语道："我们是你的思家的孩子，母亲，现在从天上回到你这里来了。"

161

The cobweb pretends to catch dewdrops and catches flies.

蛛网好像要捉露点，却捉住了苍蝇。

162

Love! When you come with the burning lamp of pain in your hand, I can see your face and know you as bliss.

爱情呀，当你手里拿着点亮了的痛苦之灯走来时，我能够看见你的脸，而且以你为幸福。

163

"The learned say that your lights will one day be no more," said the firefly to the stars. The stars made no answer.

萤火对天上的星说道:"学者说你的光明总有一天会消灭的。"
天上的星不回答它。

164

In the dusk of the evening the bird of some early dawn comes to the nest of my silence.

在黄昏的微光里,有那清晨的鸟儿来到了我的沉默的鸟巢里。

165

Thoughts pass in my mind like flocks of ducks in the sky. I hear the voice of their wings.

思想掠过我的心上,如一群野鸭飞过天空。
我听见它们鼓翼之声了。

166

The canal loves to think that rivers exist solely to supply it with water.

沟渠总喜欢想：河流的存在，是专为它供给水流的。

167

The world has kissed my soul with its pain, asking for its return in songs.

世界以它的痛苦同我接吻，而要求歌声做报酬。

168

That which oppresses me, is it my soul trying to come out in the open, or the soul of the world knocking at my heart for its entrance?

压迫着我的，到底是我的想要外出的灵魂呢，还是那世界的灵魂，敲着我心的门，想要进来呢？

169

Thought feeds itself with its own words and grows.

思想以它自己的言语喂养它自己而成长起来。

170

I have dipped the vessel of my heart into this silent hour; it has filled with love.

我把我的心之碗轻轻浸入这沉默之时刻中，它盛满了爱了。

171

Either you have work or you have not. When you have to say, "Let us do something," then begins mischief.

或者你在工作，或者你没有。

当你不得不说"让我们做些事吧"时，那么就要开始胡闹了。

172

The sunflower blushed to own the nameless flower as her kin. The sun rose and smiled on it, saying, "Are you well, my darling?"

向日葵羞于把无名的花朵看作它的同胞。

太阳升上来了，向它微笑，说道："你好么，我的宝贝儿？"

173

"Who drives me forward like fate?"
"The Myself striding on my back."

"谁如命运似的推着我向前走呢？"
"那是我自己，在身背后大跨步走着。"

174

The clouds fill the water-cups of the river, hiding themselves in the distant hills.

云把水倒在河的水杯里，它们自己却藏在远山之中。

175

I spill water from my water-jar as I walk on my way. Very little remains for my home.

我一路走去，从我的水瓶中漏出水来。

只剩下极少极少的水供我回家使用了。

176

The water in a vessel is sparkling; the water in the sea is dark. The small truth has words that are clear; the great truth has great silence.

杯中的水是光辉的；海中的水却是黑色的。

小理可以用文字来说清楚；大理却只有沉默。

177

Your smile was the flowers of your own fields, your talk was the rustle of your own mountain pines, but your heart was the woman that we all know.

你的微笑是你自己田园里的花，你的谈吐是你自己山上的松林的萧萧；但是你的心呀，却是那个女人，那个我们全都认识的女人。

178

It is the little things that I leave behind for my loved ones— great things are for everyone.

我把小小的礼物留给我所爱的人——大的礼物却留给一切的人。

179

Woman, thou hast encircled the world's heart with the depth of thy tears as the sea has the earth.

妇人呀，你用泪海包绕着世界的心，正如大海包绕着大地。

180

The sunshine greets me with a smile. The rain, his sad sister, talks to my heart.

太阳以微笑向我问候。

雨，他的忧闷的姊姊，向我的心谈话。

181

My flower of the day dropped its petals forgotten. In the evening it ripens into a golden fruit of memory.

我的昼间之花，落下它那被遗忘的花瓣。

在黄昏中，这花成熟为一颗记忆的金果。

182

I am like the road in the night listening to the footfalls of its memories in silence.

我像那夜间之路，正静悄悄地谛听着记忆的足音。

183

The evening sky to me is like a window, and a lighted lamp, and a waiting behind it.

黄昏的天空，在我看来，像一扇窗户，一盏灯火，灯火背后的一次等待。

184

He who is too busy doing good finds no time to be good.

太急于做好事的人，反而找不到时间去做好人。

185

I am the autumn cloud, empty of rain, see my fullness in the field of ripened rice.

我是秋云，空空地不载着雨水，但在成熟的稻田中，可以看见我的充实。

186

They hated and killed and men praised them. But God in shame hastens to hide its memory under the green grass.

他们嫉妒，他们残杀，人反而称赞他们。

然而上帝却害了羞，匆匆地把他的记忆埋藏在绿草下面。

187

Toes are the fingers that have forsaken their past.

脚趾乃是舍弃了其过去的手指。

188

Darkness travels towards light, but blindness towards death.

黑暗向光明旅行，但是盲者却向死亡旅行。

189

The pet dog suspects the universe for scheming to take its place.

小狗疑心大宇宙阴谋篡夺它的位置。

190

Sit still, my heart, do not raise your dust. Let the world find its way to you.

静静地坐着吧，我的心，不要扬起你的尘土。
让世界自己寻路向你走来。

191

The bow whispers to the arrow before it speeds forth—"Your freedom is mine."

弓在箭要射出之前，低声对箭说道："你的自由就是我的自由。"

192

Woman, in your laughter you have the music of the fountain of life.

妇人，在你的笑声里有着生命之泉的音乐。

193

A mind all logic is like a knife all blade. It makes the hand bleed that uses it.

全是理智的心，恰如一柄全是锋刃的刀。
它叫使用它的人手上流血。

194

God loves man's lamp-lights better than his own great stars.

神爱人间的灯光甚于他自己的大星。

195

The world is the world of wild storms kept tame with the music of beauty.

这世界乃是为美之音乐所驯服了的狂风骤雨的世界。

196

"My heart is like the golden casket of thy kiss," said the sunset cloud to the sun.

晚霞向太阳说道："我的心经了你的接吻，便似金的宝箱了。"

197

By touching you may kill, by keeping away you may possess.

接触着，你许会杀害；远离着，你许会占有。

198

The cricket's chirp and the patter of rain come to me through the dark, like the rustle of dreams from my past youth.

蟋蟀的唧唧，夜雨的淅沥，从黑暗中传到我的耳边，好似我已逝的少年时代沙沙地来到我梦境中。

199

"I have lost my dewdrop," cries the flower to the morning sky that has lost all its stars.

花朵向星辰落尽了的曙天叫道："我的露点全失落了。"

200

The burning log bursts in flame and cries, "This is my flower, my death."

燃烧着的木块，熊熊地生出火光，叫道："这是我的花朵，我的死亡。"

201

The wasp thinks that the honey-hive of the neighboring bees is too small. His neighbors ask him to build one still smaller.

黄蜂认为邻蜂储蜜之巢太小。
他的邻人要他去建筑一个更小的。

202

"I cannot keep your waves," says the bank to the river.
"Let me keep your footprints in my heart."

河岸向河流说道："我不能留住你的波浪。"
"让我保存你的足印在我心里吧。"

203

The day, with the noise of this little earth, drowns the silence of all worlds.

白日以这小小地球的喧扰，淹没了整个宇宙的沉默。

201

The song feels the infinite in the air, the picture in the earth, the poem in the air and the earth;

For its words have meaning that walks and music that soars.

歌声在空中感到无限，图画在地上感到无限，诗呢，无论在空中、在地上都是如此。

因为诗的词句含有能走动的意义与能飞翔的音乐。

205

When the sun goes down to the West, the East of his morning stands before him in silence.

太阳在西方落下时，他的早晨的东方已静悄悄地站在他面前。

206

Let me not put myself wrongly to my world and set it against me.

让我不要错误地把自己放在我的世界里而使它反对我。

207

Praise shames me, for I secretly beg for it.

荣誉使我感到惭愧，因为我暗地里求着它。

208

Let my doing nothing when I have nothing to do become untroubled in its depth of peace like the evening in the seashore when the water is silent.

当我没有什么事做时，便让我不做什么事、不受骚扰地沉入安静深处吧，一如那海水沉默时海边的暮色。

209

Maiden, your simplicity, like the blueness of the lake, reveals your depth of truth.

少女呀，你的淳朴，如湖水之碧，表现出你的真理之深邃。

210

The best does not come alone. It comes with the company of the all.

最好的东西不是独来的，
它伴了所有的东西同来。

211

God's right hand is gentle, but terrible is his left hand.

神的右手是慈爱的，但是他的左手却可怕。

212

My evening came among the alien trees and spoke in a language which my morning stars did not know.

我的晚色从陌生的树木中走来，它用我的晓星所不懂得的语言说话。

213

Night's darkness is a bag that bursts with the gold of the dawn.

夜之黑暗是一只口袋，迸出黎明的金光。

214

Our desire lends the colors of the rainbow to the mere mists and vapors of life.

我们的欲望把彩虹的颜色借给那只不过是云雾的人生。

215

God waits to win back his own flowers as gifts from man's hands.

神等待着，要从人的手上把他自己的花朵作为礼物赢得回去。

216

My sad thoughts tease me asking me their own names.

我的忧思缠扰着我，要问我它们自己的名字。

217

The service of the fruit is precious, the service of the flower is sweet, but let my service be the service of the leaves in its shade of humble devotion.

果实的事业是尊贵的，花的事业是甜美的；但是让我做叶的事业吧，叶是谦逊地、专心地垂着绿荫的。

218

My heart has spread its sails to the idle winds for the shadowy island of Anywhere.

我的心向着阑珊的风张了帆，要到无论何处的荫凉之岛去。

219

Men are cruel, but Man is kind.

独夫们是凶暴的，但人民是善良的。

220

Make me thy cup and let my fullness be for thee and for thine.

把我当做你的杯吧，让我为了你，而且为了你的人而盛满水吧。

221

The storm is like the cry of some god in pain whose love the earth refuses.

狂风暴雨像是在痛苦中的某个天神的哭声，因为他的爱情被大地所拒绝。

222

The world does not leak because death is not a crack.

世界不会流失，因为死亡并不是一个罅隙。

223

Life has become richer by the love that has been lost.

生命因为付出了的爱情而更为富足。

224

My friend, your great heart shone with the sunrise of the East like the snowy summit of a lonely hill in the dawn.

我的朋友，你伟大的心闪射出东方朝阳的光芒，正如黎明中一个积雪的孤峰。

225

The fountain of death makes the still water of life play.

死之流泉，使生的止水跳跃。

226

Those who have everything but thee, my God, laugh at those who have nothing but thyself.

那些有一切东西而没有您的人，我的上帝，在讥笑着那些没有别的东西而只有您的人呢。

227

The movement of life has its rest in its own music.

生命的运动在它自己的音乐里得到它的休息。

228

Kicks only raise dust and not crops from the earth.

踢足只能从地上扬起灰尘而不能得到收获。

229

Our names are the light that glows on the sea waves at night and then dies without leaving its signature.

我们的名字，便是夜里海波上发出的光，痕迹也不留就泯灭了。

230

Let him only see the thorns who has eyes to see the rose.

让睁眼看着玫瑰花的人也看看它的刺。

231

Set the bird's wings with gold and it will never again soar in the sky.

鸟翼上系上了黄金，这鸟便永不能再在天上翱翔了。

232

The same lotus of our clime blooms here in the alien water with the same sweetness, under another name.

我们地方的荷花又在这陌生的水上开了花，放出同样的清香，只是名字换了。

233

In heart's perspective the distance looms large.

在心的远景里，那相隔的距离显得更广阔了。

234

The moon has her light all over the sky, her dark spots to herself.

月儿把她的光明遍照在天上，却留着她的黑斑给她自己。

235

Do not say, "It is morning," and dismiss it with a name of yesterday. See it for the first time as a newborn child that has no name.

不要说"这是早晨"，别用一个"昨天"的名词把它打发掉。你第一次看到它，把它当做还没有名字的新生孩子吧。

236

Smoke boasts to the sky, and ashes to the earth, that they are brothers to the fire.

青烟对天空夸口，灰烬对大地夸口，都以为它们是火的兄弟。

237

The raindrop whispered to the jasmine, "Keep me in your heart for ever." The jasmine sighed, "Alas," and dropped to the ground.

雨点向茉莉花微语道："把我永久地留在你的心里吧。"
茉莉花叹息了一声，落在地上了。

238

Timid thoughts, do not be afraid of me, I am a poet.

惧怯的思想呀，不要怕我。
我是一个诗人。

239

The dim silence of my mind seems filled with crickets' chirp—the grey twilight of sound.

我的心在朦胧的沉默里，似乎充满了蟋蟀的鸣声——声音的灰暗的暮色。

240

Rockets, your insult to the stars follows yourself back to the earth.

爆竹呀，你对于群星的侮蔑，又跟着你自己回到地上来了。

241

Thou hast led me through my crowded travels of the day to my evening's loneliness. I wait for its meaning through the stillness of the night.

您曾经带领着我，穿过我的白天的拥挤不堪的旅程，而到达了我的黄昏的孤寂之境。

在通宵的寂静里，我等待着它的意义。

242

This life is the crossing of a sea, where we meet in the same narrow ship. In death we reach the shore and go to our different worlds.

我们的生命就似渡过一个大海，我们都相聚在这个狭小的舟中。

死时，我们便到了岸，各往各的世界去了。

243

The stream of truth flows through its channels of mistakes.

真理之川从它的错误之沟渠中流过。

244

My heart is homesick today for the one sweet hour across the sea of time.

今天我的心是在想家了，在想着那跨过时间之海的那一个甜蜜的时候。

245

The bird-song is the echo of the morning light back from the earth.

鸟的歌声是曙光从大地反响过去的回声。

246

"Are you too proud to kiss me?" the morning light asks the buttercup.

晨光问毛莨道："你是骄傲得不肯和我接吻么？"

247

"How may I sing to thee and worship, O Sun?" asked the little flower.

"By the simple silence of thy purity," answered the sun.

小花问道："我要怎样地对你唱，怎样地崇拜你呢？太阳呀？"

太阳答道："只要用你的纯洁的素朴的沉默。"

248

Man is worse than an animal when he is an animal.

当人是兽时，他比兽还坏。

249

Dark clouds become heaven's flowers when kissed by light.

黑云受光的接吻时便变成天上的花朵。

250

Let not the sword-blade mock its handle for being blunt.

不要让刀锋讥笑它柄子的拙钝。

251

The night's silence, like a deep lamp, is burning with the light of its Milky Way.

夜的沉默，如一个深深的灯盏，银河便是它燃着的灯光。

252

Around the sunny island of life swells day and night death's limitless song of the sea.

死像大海的无限的歌声，日夜冲击着生命的光明岛的四周。

253

Is not this mountain like a flower, with its petals of hills, drinking the sunlight?

花瓣似的山峰在饮着日光，这山岂不像一朵花吗？

254

The real with its meaning read wrong and emphasis misplaced is the unreal.

"真实"的含义被误解，轻重被倒置，那就成了"不真实"。

255

Find your beauty, my heart, from the world's movement, like the boat that has the grace of the wind and the water.

我的心呀，从世界的流动中找你的美吧，正如那小船得到风与水的优美似的。

256

The eyes are not proud of their sight but of their eyeglasses.

眼不以能视来骄人，却以它们的眼镜来骄人。

257

I live in this little world of mine and am afraid to make it the least less. Lift me into thy world and let me have the freedom gladly to lose my all.

我住在我的这个小小世界里，生怕使它再缩小一丁点儿。把我抬举到您的世界里去吧，让我有高高兴兴地失去我的一切的自由。

258

The false can never grow into truth by growing in power.

虚伪永远不能凭借它生长在权力中而变成真实。

259

My heart, with its lapping waves of song, longs to caress this green world of the sunny day.

我的心，同着它的歌的拍拍舐岸的波浪，渴望着要抚爱这个阳光熙和的绿色世界。

260

Wayside grass, love the star, then your dreams will come out in flowers.

道旁的草，爱那天上的星吧，你的梦境便可在花朵里实现了。

261

Let your music, like a sword, pierce the noise of the market to its heart.

让你的音乐如一柄利刃，直刺入市井喧扰的心中吧。

262

The trembling leaves of this tree touch my heart like the fingers of an infant child.

这树的颤动之叶，触动着我的心，像一个婴儿的手指。

263

The little flower lies in the dust. It sought the path of the butterfly.

小花睡在尘土里。
它寻求蛱蝶走的道路。

264

I am in the world of the roads. The night comes. Open thy
gate, thou world of the home.

我是在道路纵横的世界上。

夜来了。打开您的门吧，家之世界呵！

265

I have sung the songs of thy day. In the evening let me carry thy
lamp through the stormy path.

我已经唱过了您的白天的歌。

在黄昏时候，让我拿着您的灯走过风雨飘摇的道路吧。

266

I do not ask thee into the house. Come into my infinite
loneliness, my Lover.

我不要求你进我的屋里。

你到我无量的孤寂里来吧，我的爱人！

267

Death belongs to life as birth does. The walk is in the raising of the foot as in the laying of it down.

死亡隶属于生命，正与生一样。

举足是走路，正如落足也是走路。

268

I have learnt the simple meaning of thy whispers in flowers and sunshine—teach me to know thy words in pain and death.

我已经学会了你在花与阳光里微语的意义。——再教我明白你在苦与死中所说的话吧。

269

The night's flower was late when the morning kissed her, she shivered and sighed and dropped to the ground.

夜的花朵来晚了，当早晨吻着她时，她战栗着，叹息了一声，萎落在地上了。

270

Through the sadness of all things I hear the crooning of the Eternal Mother.

从万物的愁苦中，我听见了"永恒母亲"的呻吟。

271

I came to your shore as a stranger, I lived in your house as a guest, I leave your door as a friend, my earth.

大地呀，我到你岸上时是一个陌生人，住在你屋内时是一个宾客，离开你的门时是一个朋友。

272

Let my thoughts come to you, when I am gone, like the afterglow of sunset at the margin of starry silence.

当我去时，让我的思想到你那里来，如那夕阳的余光，映在沉默的星天的边上。

273

Light in my heart the evening star of rest and then let the night whisper to me of love.

在我的心头燃点起那休憩的黄昏星吧，然后让黑夜向我微语着爱情。

274

I am a child in the dark. I stretch my hands through the coverlet of night for thee, Mother.

我是一个在黑暗中的孩子。

我从夜的被单里向您伸出我的双手，母亲。

275

The day of work is done. Hide my face in your arms, Mother.

Let me dream.

白天的工作完了。把我的脸掩藏在您的臂间吧，母亲。

让我入梦吧。

276

The lamp of meeting burns long; it goes out in a moment at the parting.

集会时的灯光，点了很久，会散时，灯便立刻灭了。

277

One word keep for me in thy silence, O World, when I am dead, "I have loved."

当我死时，世界呀，请在你的沉默中，替我留着"我已经爱过了"这句话吧。

278

We live in this world when we love it.

我们在热爱世界时便生活在这世界上。

279

Let the dead have the immortality of fame, but the living the immortality of love.

让死者有那不朽的名，但让生者有那不朽的爱。

280

I have seen thee as the half-awakened child sees his mother in the dusk of the dawn and then smiles and sleeps again.

我看见你，像那半醒的婴孩在黎明的微光里看见他的母亲，于是微笑而又睡去了。

281

I shall die again and again to know that life is inexhaustible.

我将死了又死，以明白生是无穷无尽的。

282

While I was passing with the crowd in the road I saw thy smile from the balcony and I sang and forgot all noise.

当我和拥挤的人群一同在路上走过时，我看见您从阳台上送过来的微笑，我歌唱着，忘却了所有的喧哗。

283

Love is life in its fullness like the cup with its wine.

爱就是充实了的生命，正如盛满了酒的酒杯。

284

They light their own lamps and sing their own words in their temples. But the birds sing thy name in thine own morning light——for thy name is joy.

他们点了他们自己的灯，在他们的寺院内，吟唱他们自己的话语。

但是小鸟们却在你的晨光中，唱着你的名字——因为你的名字便是快乐。

285

Lead me in the center of thy silence to fill my heart with songs.

领我到您的沉寂的中心，使我的心充满了歌吧。

286

Let them live who choose in their own hissing world of fireworks. My heart longs for thy stars, my God.

让那些选择了他们自己的焰火咝咝的世界的，就生活在那里吧。我的心渴望着您的繁星，我的上帝。

287

Love's pain sang round my life like the unplumbed sea, and love's joy sang like birds in its flowering groves.

爱的痛苦环绕着我的一生，像汹涌的大海似的唱着；而爱的快乐却像鸟儿们在花林里似的唱着。

288

Put out the lamp when thou wishest. I shall know thy darkness and shall love it.

假如您愿意，您就熄了灯吧。
我将明白您的黑暗，而且将喜爱它。

289

When I stand before thee at the day's end thou shalt see my scars and know that I had my wounds and also my healing.

当我在那日子的终了，站在您的面前时，您将看见我的伤疤，而知道我有我的许多创伤，但也有我的医治的法儿。

290

Some day I shall sing to thee in the sunrise of some other world, "I have seen thee before in the light of the earth, in the love of man."

总有一天，我要在别的世界的晨光里对你唱道："我以前在地球的光里，在人的爱里，已经见过你了。"

291

Clouds come floating into my life from other days no longer to shed rain or usher storm but to give color to my sunset sky.

从别的日子里飘浮到我的生命里的云，不再落下雨点或引起风暴了，却只给予我的夕阳的天空以色彩。

292

Truth raises against itself the storm that scatters its seeds broadcast.

真理引起了反对它自己的狂风骤雨，那场风雨吹散了真理的广播的种子。

293

The storm of the last night has crowned this morning with golden peace.

昨夜的风雨给今日的早晨戴上了金色的和平。

294

Truth seems to come with its final word; and the final word gives birth to its next.

真理仿佛带了它的结论而来，而那结论却产生了它的第二个。

295

Blessed is he whose fame does not outshine his truth.

他是有福的，因为他的名望并没有比他的真实更光亮。

296

Sweetness of thy name fills my heart when I forget mine—like thy morning sun when the mist is melted.

您的名字的甜蜜充溢着我的心，而我忘掉了我自己的——就像您的早晨的太阳升起时，那大雾便消失了。

297

The silent night has the beauty of the mother and the clamorous day of the child.

静悄悄的黑夜具有母亲的美丽，而吵闹的白天具有孩子的美。

298

The world loved man when he smiled. The world became afraid of him when he laughed.

当人微笑时，世界爱了他；当他大笑时，世界便怕他了。

299

God waits for man to regain his childhood in wisdom.

神等待着人在智慧中重新获得童年。

300

Let me feel this world as thy love taking form, then my love will help it.

让我感到这个世界乃是您的爱的成形吧，那么，我的爱也将帮助着它。

301

Thy sunshine smiles upon the winter days of my heart, never doubting of its spring flowers.

您的阳光对着我的心头的冬天微笑着，从来不怀疑它的春天的花朵。

302

God kisses the finite in his love and man the infinite.

神在他的爱里吻着"有涯"，而人却吻着"无涯"。

303

Thou crossest desert lands of barren years to reach the moment of fulfillment.

您越过不毛之地的沙漠而到达了圆满的时刻。

304

God's silence ripens man's thoughts into speech.

神的静默使人的思想成熟而为语言。

305

Thou wilt find, Eternal Traveler, marks of thy footsteps across my songs.

"永恒的旅客"呀，你可以在我的歌中找到你的足迹。

306

Let me not shame thee, Father, who displayest thy glory in thy children.

让我不至羞辱您吧，父亲，您在您的孩子们身上显现出您的光荣。

307

Cheerless is the day, the light under frowning clouds is like a punished child with traces of tears on its pale cheeks, and the cry of the wind is like the cry of a wounded world. But I know I am traveling to meet my Friend.

这一天是不快活的。光在蹙额的云下，如一个被责打的儿童，灰白的脸上留着泪痕；风又叫号着，似一个受伤的世界的哭声。但是我知道，我正跋涉着去会我的朋友。

308

Tonight there is a stir among the palm leaves, a swell in the sea, Full Moon, like the heart-throb of the world. From what unknown sky hast thou carried in thy silence the aching secret of love?

今天晚上棕榈叶在嚓嚓地作响，海上有大浪，满月呵，就像世界在心脉悸跳。从什么不可知的天空，您在您的沉默里带来了爱的痛苦的秘密？

309

I dream of a star, an island of light, where I shall be born and in the depth of its quickening leisure my life will ripen its works like the rice-field in the autumn sun.

我梦见一颗星，一个光明岛屿，我将在那里出生。在它快速的闲暇深处，我的生命将成熟它的事业，像秋天阳光下的稻田。

310

The smell of the wet earth in the rain rises like a great chant of praise from the voiceless multitude of the insignificant.

雨中的湿土的气息，就像从渺小的无声的群众那里来的一阵巨大的赞美歌声。

311

That love can ever lose is a fact that we cannot accept as truth.

说爱情会失去的那句话，乃是我们不能够当做真理来接受的一个事实。

312

We shall know some day that death can never rob us of that which our soul has gained, for her gains are one with herself.

我们将有一天会明白，死永远不能够夺去我们的灵魂所获得的东西。因为她所获得的，和她自己是一体。

313

God comes to me in the dusk of my evening with the flowers from my past kept fresh in his basket.

神在我的黄昏的微光中，带着花到我这里来。这些花都是我过去的，在他的花篮中还保存得很新鲜。

314

When all the strings of my life will be tuned, my Master, then at every touch of thine will come out the music of love.

主呀，当我的生之琴弦都已调得谐和时，你的手的一弹一奏，都可以发出爱的乐声来。

315

Let me live truly, my Lord, so that death to me become true.

让我真真实实地活着吧，我的上帝。这样，死对于我也就成了真实的了。

316

Man's history is waiting in patience for the triumph of the insulted man.

人类的历史在很忍耐地等待着被侮辱者的胜利。

317

I feel thy gaze upon my heart this moment like the sunny silence of the morning upon the lonely field whose harvest is over.

我这一刻感到你的眼光正落在我的心上，像那早晨阳光中的沉默落在已收获的孤寂的田野上一样。

318

I long for the Island of Songs across this heaving Sea of Shouts.

在这喧哗的波涛起伏的海中，我渴望着咏歌之鸟。

319

The prelude of the night is commenced in the music of the sunset, in its solemn hymn to the ineffable dark.

夜的序曲是开始于夕阳西下的音乐，开始于它对难以形容的黑暗所作的庄严的赞歌。

320

I have scaled the peak and found no shelter in fame's bleak and barren height. Lead me, my Guide, before the light fades, into the valley of quiet where life's harvest mellows into golden wisdom.

我攀登上高峰，发现在名誉的荒芜不毛的高处，简直找不到一个遮身之地。我的引导者呵，领导着我在光明逝去之前，进到沉静的山谷里去吧。在那里，一生的收获将会成熟为黄金的智慧。

321

Things look phantastic in this dimness of the dusk——the spires whose bases are lost in the dark and tree-tops like blots of ink. I shall wait for the morning and wake up to see thy city in the light.

在这个黄昏的朦胧里，好些东西看来都仿佛是幻象一般——尖塔的底层在黑暗里消失了，树顶像是墨水的模糊的斑点似的。我将等待着黎明，而当我醒来的时候，就会看到在光明里的您的城市。

322

I have suffered and despaired and known death and I am glad that I am in this great world.

我曾经受过苦，曾经失望过，曾经体会过"死亡"，于是我以我在这伟大的世界里为乐。

323

There are tracts in my life that are bare and silent. They are the open spaces where my busy days had their light and air.

在我的一生里，也有贫乏和沉默的地域。它们是我忙碌的日子得到日光与空气的几片空旷之地。

324

Release me from my unfulfilled past clinging to me from behind making death difficult.

我的未完成的过去，从后边缠绕到我身上，使我难于死去。请从它那里释放了我吧。

325

Let this be my last word, that I trust in thy love.

"我相信你的爱。"让这句话做我的最后的话。

新月集

使生如夏花之绚烂，死如秋叶之静美。

译者自序

　　我对于泰戈尔（R. Tagore）的诗最初发生浓厚的兴趣，是在第一次读《新月集》的时候。那时离现在将近五年，许地山君坐在我家的客厅里，长发垂到两肩，很神秘地在黄昏的微光中，对我谈到泰戈尔的事。他说，他在缅甸时，看到泰戈尔的画像，又听人讲到他，便买了他的诗集来读。过了几天，我到许地山君的宿舍里去。他说："我拿一本泰戈尔的诗选送给你。"他便到书架上去找那本诗集。我立在窗前，四围静悄悄的，只有水池中喷泉的潺潺的声音。我静静地等候读那本美丽的书。他不久便从书架上取下很小的一本绿纸面的书来。他说："这是一个日本人选的泰戈尔诗，你先拿去看看。泰戈尔不久前曾到过日本。"我坐了车回家，在归程中，借着新月与市灯的微光，约略地把它翻看了一遍。最使我喜欢的是其中所选的几首《新月集》的诗。那一夜，在灯下又看了一次。第二天，地山见我时，问道：

"你最喜欢哪几首？"我说："《新月集》的几首。"他隔了几天，又拿了一本很美丽的书给我，他说："这就是《新月集》。"从那时以后，《新月集》便常在我的书桌上。直到现在，我还时时把它翻开来读。

我译《新月集》，也是受地山君的鼓励。有一天，他把他所译的《吉檀迦利》的几首诗给我看，都是用古文译的。我说："译得很好，但似乎太古奥了。"他说："这一类的诗，应该用这个古奥的文体译。至于《新月集》，却又须用新妍流露的文字译。我想译《吉檀迦利》，你为何不译《新月集》呢？"于是我与他约，我们同时动手译这两部书。此后二年中，他的《吉檀迦利》固未译成，我的《新月集》也时译时辍。直至《小说月报》改革后，我才把自己所译的《新月集》在它上面发表了几首。地山译的《吉檀迦利》却始终没有再译下去。已译的几首也始终不肯拿出来发表。后来王独清君译的《新月集》也出版了，我更懒得把自己的译下去。许多朋友却时时催我把这个工作做完。他们都说，王君的译文太不容易懂了，似乎有再译的必要。那时我正有选译泰戈尔诗的计划，便一方面把旧译的稿整理一下，一方面参考了王君的译文，又新译了八九首出来，结果便成了现在的这个译本。原集里还有九首诗，因为我不大喜欢它们，所以没有译出来①。

我喜欢《新月集》，如我之喜欢安徒生的童话。安徒生的文字美丽而富有诗趣，他有一种不可测的魔力，能把我们从忙扰的人世间带到美丽和平的花的世界、虫的世界、人鱼的世界里去；能使我们忘了一切艰苦的境遇，随了他走进有静的方池的绿水、有美的挂在黄昏的

---

① 本书的《新月集》，是增补完备的全译本。——编者注

天空的雨后弧虹等等的天国里去。《新月集》也具有这种不可测的魔力。它把我们从怀疑贪望的成人的世界，带到秀嫩天真的儿童的新月之国里去。我们忙着费时间在计算数字，它却能使我们重又回到坐在泥土里以枯枝断梗为戏的时代；我们忙着入海采珠，掘山寻金，它却能使我们在心里重温着在海滨以贝壳为餐具，以落叶为舟，以绿草的露点为圆珠的儿童的梦。总之，我们只要一翻开它来，便立刻如得到两只有魔术的翼膀，可以使自己从现实的苦闷的境地里飞翔到美静天真的儿童国里去。

有许多人以为《新月集》是一部写给儿童看的书。这是他们受了广告上附注的"儿歌"（"Child Poems"）二字的暗示的缘故。实际上，《新月集》虽然未尝没有几首儿童可以看得懂的诗歌，而泰戈尔之写这些诗，却决非为儿童而作的。它并不是一部写给儿童读的诗歌集，乃是一部叙述儿童心理、儿童生活的最好的诗歌集。这正如俄国许多民众小说家所作的民众小说，并不是为民众而作，而是写民众的生活的作品一样。我们如果认清了这一点，便不会无端地引起什么怀疑与什么争论了。

我的译文自己很不满意，但似乎还很忠实，且不至看不懂。

读者的一切指教，我都欢迎地承受。

我最后应该向许地山君表示谢意。他除了鼓励我以外，在这个译本写好时，还曾为我校读了一次。

郑振铎　十二，八，二十二。

再版自序

《新月集》译本出版后，曾承几位朋友批评，这是我要对他们表白十二分的谢意的。现在乘再版的机会，把第一版中所有错误，就所能觉察到的，改正一下。读者诸君及朋友们如果更有所发现，希望他们能够告诉我，俾得于第三版时再校正。

郑振铎　十三,三,二十。

THE HOME

I paced alone on the road across the field while the sunset was hiding its last gold like a miser.

The daylight sank deeper and deeper into the darkness, and the widowed land, whose harvest had been reaped, lay silent.

Suddenly a boy's shrill voice rose into the sky. He traversed the dark unseen, leaving the track of his song across the hush of the evening.

His village home lay there at the end of the waste land, beyond the sugar—cane field, hidden among the shadows of the banana and the slender areca palm, the cocoa—nut and the dark green jack—fruit tress.

I stopped for a moment in my lonely way under the starlight, and saw spread before me the darkened earth surrounding with her arms countless homes furnished with cradles and beds, mothers' hearts and evening lamps, and young lives glad with a gladness that knows nothing of its value for the world.

家庭

　　我独自在横跨过田地的路上走着。夕阳像一个守财奴似的，正藏起它的最后的金子。

　　白昼更加深沉地投入黑暗之中，那已经收割了的孤寂的田地，默默地躺在那里。

　　天空里突然升起了一个男孩子的尖锐的歌声，他穿过看不见的黑暗，留下他的歌声的辙痕跨过黄昏的静谧。

　　他的乡村的家坐落在荒凉的土地的边上，在甘蔗田的后面，躲藏在香蕉树、瘦长的槟榔树、椰子树和深绿色的贾克果树的阴影里。

　　我在星光下独自走着的路上停留了一会儿，我看见黑沉沉的大地展开在我的面前，用她的手臂拥抱着无量数的家庭，在那些家庭里，有着摇篮和床铺，母亲们的心和夜晚的灯，还有年轻轻的生命。他们满心欢乐，却浑然不知这样的欢乐对于世界的价值。

ON THE SEASHORE

On the seashore of endless worlds children meet.

The infinite sky is motionless overhead and the restless water is boisterous. On the seashore of endless worlds the children meet with shouts and dances.

They build their houses with sand, and they play with empty shells. With withered leaves they weave their boats and smilingly float them on the vast deep. Children have their play on the seashore of worlds.

They know not how to swim, they know not how to cast nets. Pearl—fishers dive for pearls, merchants sail in their ships, while children gather pebbles and scatter them again. They seek not for hidden treasures, they know not how to cast nets.

The sea surges up with laughter, and pale gleams the smile of the sea—beach. Death—dealing waves sing meaningless ballads to the children, even like a mother while rocking her baby's cradle. The sea plays with children, and pale gleams the smile of the sea beach.

On the seashore of endless worlds children meet. Tempest

roams in the pathless sky, ships are wrecked in the trackless water, death is abroad and children play. On the seashore of endless worlds is the great meeting of children.

海边

小孩子们汇集在这无边无际的世界的海边。

无限的天穹静止地临于头上，不息的海水在足下汹涌着。小孩子们汇集在这无边无际的世界的海边，叫着跳着。

他们拿沙来建筑房屋，拿空贝壳来做游戏。他们把落叶编成了船，微笑地把他们放到广大的深海上。小孩子们在这世界的海边，做他们的游戏。

他们不知道怎样泅水，他们不知道怎样放网。采珠的人为了珠下水，商人在他们的船上航行，小孩子们却只把小圆石聚了又散。他们不搜求藏宝；他们不知道怎样放网。

海水带着笑掀起波浪，海边也淡淡地闪耀着微笑。致人死命的波涛，对着小孩子们唱无意义的歌曲，很像一个摇动她孩子的摇篮时的母亲，海水和小孩子们一同游戏，海边也淡淡地闪耀着微笑。

　　小孩子们汇集在这无边无际的海边。狂风暴雨飘游在无辙迹的天空上，航船沉碎在无辙迹的海水里，死正在外面走着，小孩子们却在游戏。在这无边无际的世界的海边上，小孩子们大汇集着。

THE SOURCE

The sleep that flits on baby's eyes—does anybody know from where it comes? Yes, there is a rumour that it has its dwelling where, in the fairy village among shadows of the forest dimly lit with glow-worms, there hang two shy buds of enchantment. From there it comes to kiss baby's eyes.

The smile that flickers on baby's lips when he sleeps—does anybody know where it was born? Yes, there is a rumour that a young pale beam of a crescent moon touched the edge of a vanishing autumn cloud, and there the smile was first born in the dream of a dew-washed morningthe smile that flickers on baby's lips when he sleeps.

The sweet, soft freshness that blooms on baby's limbs—does

anybody know where it was hidden so long? Yes, when the mother was a young girl it lay pervading her heart in tender and silent mystery of love—the sweet, soft freshness that has bloomed on baby's limbs.

来源

流泛在孩子两眼的睡眠，——有谁知道他是从什么地方来的？是的，有个谣传，说他是住在萤火虫朦胧地照着的林影里的仙村里，在那个地方挂着两个迷人的悃怯的蓓蕾。他便是从那个地方来吻着孩子的两眼的。

当孩子睡时，微笑在他唇上浮动着，——有谁知道他是从什么地方生出来的？是的，有个谣传，说，一线新月的幼嫩的清光，触着将消未消的秋云边上，微笑便在那个地方初生在一个浴在清露里的早晨的梦中了。

甜蜜柔嫩的新鲜情景，在孩子的四肢上展放着，——有谁知道他在什么地方藏得这样久？是的，当母亲是一个少女的时候，他已在爱的温柔而沉静的神秘中，潜伏在她的心里。——甜蜜柔嫩的新鲜情景，在孩子的四肢上展放着。

BABYS WAY

If baby only wanted to, he could fly up to heaven this moment.

It is not for nothing that he does not leave us.

He loves to rest his head on mother's bosom, and cannot ever bear to lose sight of her.

Baby knows all manner of wise words, though few on earth can understand their meaning.

It is not for nothing that he never wants to speak.

The one thing he wants is to learn mother's words from mother's lips. That is why he looks so innocent.

Baby had a heap of gold and pearls, yet he came like a beggar on to this earth.

It is not for nothing he came in such a disguise.

This dear little naked mendicant pretends to be utterly helpless, so that he may beg for mother's wealth of love.

Baby was so free from every tie in the land of the tiny crescent moon.

It was not for nothing he gave up his freedom.

He knows that there is room for endless joy in mother's little corner of a heart, and it is sweeter far than liberty to be caught and pressed in her dear arms.

Baby never knew how to cry. He dwelt in the land of perfect bliss.

It is not for nothing he has chosen to shed tears.

Though with the smile of his dear face he draws mother's yearning heart to him, yet his little cries over tiny troubles weave the double bond of pity and love.

孩童之道

只要孩童愿意，他此刻便可飞上天去。

他所以不离开我们，并不是没有缘故。

他爱把他的头倚在妈妈的胸间，他即使是一刻不见她，也是不行的。

孩童知道各式各样的聪明话，虽然世间的人很少懂得这些话的意义。

他所以永不想说，并不是没有缘故。

他所要做的一件事，就是要学习从妈妈的嘴唇里说出来的话。那就是他所以看来这样天真的缘故。

孩童有成堆的黄金与珠子，但他到这个世界上来，却像一个乞丐。

他所以这样假装了来，并不是没有缘故。

这个可爱的小小的裸着身体的乞丐，所以假装着完全无助的样子，便是想要乞求妈妈的爱的财富。

孩童在纤小的新月的世界里，是一切束缚都没有的。

他所以放弃了他的自由，并不是没有缘故。

他知道有无穷的快乐藏在妈妈的心的小小一隅里，被妈妈亲爱的手臂拥抱着，其甜美远胜过自由。

孩童永不知道如何哭泣。他所住的是完全的乐土。

他所以要流泪，并不是没有缘故。

虽然他用了可爱的脸儿上的微笑，引逗得他妈妈的热切的心向着他，然而他的因为细故而发的小小的哭声，却编成了怜与爱的双重约束的带子。

THE UNHEEDED PAGEANT

Ah, who was it coloured that little frock, my child, and covered your sweet limbs with that little red tunic?

You have come out in the morning to play in the courtyard, tottering and tumbling as you run.

But who was it coloured that little frock, my child?

What is it makes you laugh, my little life—bud?

Mother smiles at you standing on the threshold.

She claps her hands and her bracelets jingle, and you dance with your bamboo stick in your hand like a tiny little shepherd.

But what is it makes you laugh, my little life—bud?

O, beggar, what do you beg for, clinging to your mother's neck with both your hands?

O, greedy heart, shall I pluck the world like a fruit from the sky to place it on your little rosy palm?

O, beggar, what are you begging for?

The wind carries away in glee the tinkling of your anklet bells.

The sun smiles and watches your toilet.

The sky watches over you when you sleep in your mother's arms, and the morning comes tiptoe to your bed and kisses your eyes.

The wind carries away in glee the tinkling of your anklet bells.

The fairy mistress of dreams is coming towards you, flying through the twilight sky.

The world-mother keeps her seat by you in your mother's heart.

He who plays his music to the stars is standing at your window with his flute.

And the fairy mistress of dreams is coming towards you, flying through the twilight sky.

不被注意的花饰

呵，谁给那件小外衫染上颜色的，我的孩子？谁使你的温软的肢体穿上那件红色小外衫的？

你在早晨就跑出来到天井里玩儿，你，跑着就像摇摇欲跌似的。

但是谁给那件小外衫染上颜色的，我的孩子？

什么事叫你大笑起来的，我的小小的命芽儿？

妈妈站在门边，微笑地望着你。

她拍着双手，她的手镯叮当地响着；你手里拿着你的竹竿儿在跳舞，活像一个小小的牧童儿。

但是什么事叫你大笑起来的，我的小小的命芽儿？

喔，乞丐，你双手攀搂住妈妈的头颈，要乞讨些什么？

喔，贪得无厌的心，要我把整个世界从天上摘下来，像摘一个果子似的，把它放在你的一双小小的玫瑰色的手掌上么？

喔，乞丐，你要乞讨些什么？

风高兴地带走了你踝铃的叮当。

太阳微笑着，望着你的打扮。

当你睡在你妈妈的臂弯里时，天空在上面望着你，而早晨蹑手蹑脚地走到你的床跟前，吻着你的双眼。

风高兴地带走了你踝铃的叮当。

仙乡里的梦婆飞过朦胧的天空，向你飞来。

在你妈妈的心头上，那世界母亲，正和你坐在一块儿。

他，向星星奏乐的人，正拿着他的横笛，站在你的窗边。

仙乡里的梦婆飞过朦胧的天空，向你飞来。

SLEEP-STEALER

Who stole sleep from baby's eyes? I must know.

Clasping her pitcher to her waist, mother went to fetch water from the village near by.

It was noon. The children's playtime was over; the ducks in the pond were silent.

The shepherd boy lay asleep under the shadow of the banyan tree.

The crane stood grave and still in the swamp near the mango grove.

In the meanwhile the Sleep-stealer came and, snatching sleep from baby's eyes, flew away.

When mother came back she found baby travelling the room over on all fours.

Who stole sleep from our baby's eyes? I must know. I must find her and chain her up.

I must look into that dark cave, where, through boulders and scowling stones, trickles a tiny stream.

I must search in the drowsy shade of the bakula grove, where pigeons coo in their corner, and fairies' anklets tinkle in the stillness of starry nights.

In the evening I will peep into the whispering silence of the bamboo forest, where fire−flies squander their light, and will ask every creature I meet, "Can anybody tell me where the Sleep−stealer lives?"

Who stole sleep from baby's eyes? I must know.

Shouldn't I give her a good lesson if I could only catch her!

I would raid her nest and see where she hoards all her stolen sleep.

I would plunder it all, and carry it home.

I would bind her two wings securely, set her on the bank of the river, and then let her play at fishing with a reed among the rushes and water−lilies.

When the marketing is over in the evening, and the village children sit in their mothers' laps, then the night birds will mockingly din her ears with:

"Whose sleep will you steal now?"

偷睡眠者

谁从孩子的眼里把睡眠偷了去呢？我一定要知道。

　　妈妈把她的水罐挟在腰间，走到近村汲水去了。

　　这是正午的时候。孩子们游戏的时间已经过去了；池中的鸭子沉默无声。

　　牧童躺在榕树的荫下睡着了。

　　白鹤庄重而安静地立在芒果树边的泥泽里。

　　就在这个时候，偷睡眠者跑来从孩子的两眼里捉住睡眠，便飞去了。

　　当妈妈回来时，她看见孩子四肢着地地在屋里爬着。

　　谁从孩子的眼里把睡眠偷了去呢？我一定要知道。我一定要找到她，把她锁起来。

　　我一定要向那个黑洞里张望。在这个洞里，有一道小泉从圆的和有皱纹的石上滴下来。

　　我一定要到醉花①林中的沉寂的树影里搜寻。在这林中鸽子在它们住的地方咕咕地叫着，仙女的脚环在繁星满天的静夜里叮当地响着。

　　我要在黄昏时，向静静的萧萧的竹林里窥望。在这林中，萤火虫闪闪地耗费它们的光明，只要遇见一个人，我便要问他，"谁能告诉我偷睡眠者住在什么地方？"

　　谁从孩子的眼里把睡眠偷了去呢？我一定要知道。

　　只要我能捉住她，怕不会给她一顿好教训！

　　我要闯入她的巢穴，看她把所有偷来的睡眠藏在什么地方。

---

① 印度传说：美女口中吐出香液，此花始开。

　　我要把它都夺了来，带回家去。

　　我要把她的双翼缚得紧紧的，把她放在河边，然后叫她拿一根芦苇，在灯心草和睡莲间钓鱼为戏。

　　当黄昏，街上已经收了市，村里的孩子们都坐在妈妈的膝上时，夜鸟便会讥笑地在她耳边说：

　　"你现在还想偷谁的睡眠呢？"

THE BEGINNING

"Where have I come from, where did you pick me up?" the baby asked its mother.

She answered half crying, half laughing, and clasping the baby to her breast—

"You were hidden in my heart as its desire, my darling.

You were in the dolls of my childhood's games; and when with clay I made the image of my god every morning, I made and unmade you then.

You were enshrined with our household deity, in his worship I worshipped you.

In all my hopes and my loves, in my life, in the life of my mother you have lived.

In the lap of the deathless Spirit who rules our home you have been nursed for ages.

When in girlhood my heart was opening its petals, you hovered as a fragrance about it.

Your tender softness bloomed in my youthful limbs, like a glow in the sky before the sunrise.

Heaven's first darling, twin-born with the morning light, you have floated down the stream of the world's life, and at last you have stranded on my heart.

As I gaze on your face, mystery overwhelms me; you who belong to all have become mine.

For fear of losing you I hold you tight to my breast. What magic has snared the world's treasure in these slender arms of mine?"

开始

"我是从哪儿来的？你，在哪儿把我捡起来的？"孩子问他的妈妈说。

她把孩子紧紧地搂在胸前，半哭半笑地答道——

"你曾被我当做心愿藏在我的心里，我的宝贝。

"你曾存在于我孩童时代玩的泥娃娃身上；每天早晨我用泥土塑造我的神像，那时我反复地塑了又捏碎了的就是你。

"你曾和我们的家庭守护神一同受到祀奉，我崇拜家神时也就崇拜了你。

"你曾活在我所有的希望和爱情里，活在我的生命里，我母亲的生命里。

"在主宰着我们家庭的不死的精灵的膝上，你已经被抚育了好多代了。

"当我做女孩子的时候，我的心的花瓣儿张开，你就像一股花香似的散发出来。

"你的软软的温柔，在我青春的肢体上开花了，像太阳出来之前的天空里的一片曙光。

"上天的第一宠儿，晨曦的孪生兄弟，你从世界的生命的溪流浮泛而下，终于停泊在我的心头。

"当我凝视你的脸蛋儿的时候，神秘之感湮没了我；你这属于一切人的，竟成了我的。

"为了怕失掉你，我把你紧紧地搂在胸前。是什么魔术把这世界的宝贝引到我这双纤小的手臂里来的呢？"

BABYS WORLD

I wish I could take a quiet corner in the heart of my baby's very own world.

I know it has stars that talk to him, and a sky that stoops down to his face to amuse him with its silly clouds and rainbows.

Those who make believe to be dumb, and look as if they never could move, come creeping to his window with their stories and with trays crowded with bright toys.

I wish I could travel by the road that crosses baby's mind, and out beyond all bounds;

Where messengers run errands for no cause between the kingdoms of kings of no history;

Where Reason makes kites of her laws and flies them, and Truth sets Fact free from its fetters.

孩子的世界

我愿我能在我孩子自己的世界的中心，占一角清净地。

我知道有星星同他说话，天空也在他面前垂下，用它呆呆的云朵和彩虹来娱悦他。

那些大家以为他是哑的人，那些看上去像是永不会走动的人，都带了他们的故事，捧了满装着五颜六色的玩具的盘子，匍匐地来到他的窗前。

我愿我能在横过孩子心中的道路上游行，解脱了一切的束缚；

在那儿，使者奉了无所谓的使命奔走于无史的诸王的王国间；

在那儿，理智以它的法律造为纸鸢而飞放，真理也使事实从桎梏中自由了。

WHEN AND WHY

When I bring you coloured toys, my child, I understand why there is such a play of colours on clouds, on water, and why flowers are painted in tints—when I give coloured toys to you, my child.

When I sing to make you dance, I truly know why there is music in leaves, and why waves send their chorus of voices to the heart of the listening earth—when I sing to make you dance.

When I bring sweet things to your greedy hands, I know why there is honey in the cup of the flower, and why fruits are secretly filled with sweet juice—when I bring sweet things to your greedy hands.

When I kiss your face to make you smile, my darling, I surely understand what pleasure streams from the sky in morning light, and what delight the summer breeze brings to my body—when I kiss you to make you smile.

时候与原因

当我给你五颜六色的玩具的时候，我的孩子，我明白了为什么云上水上是这样的色彩缤纷，为什么花朵上染上绚烂的颜色的原因了——当我给你五颜六色的玩具的时候，我的孩子。

当我唱着使你跳舞的时候，我真的知道了为什么树叶儿响着音乐，为什么波浪把它们的合唱的声音送进静听着的大地的心头的原因了——当我唱着使你跳舞的时候。

当我把糖果送到你贪得无厌的双手上的时候，我知道了为什么在花萼里会有蜜，为什么水果里会秘密地充溢了甜汁的原因了——当我把糖果送到你贪得无厌的双手上的时候。

当我吻着你的脸蛋儿叫你微笑的时候，我的宝贝，我的确明白了在晨光里从天上流下来的是什么样的快乐，而夏天的微风吹拂在我身体上的又是什么样的爽快——当我吻着你的脸蛋儿叫你微笑的时候。

DEFAMATION

Why are those tears in your eyes, my child?

How horrid of them to be always scolding you for nothing!

You have stained your fingers and face with ink while writing——is that why they call you dirty?

O, fie! Would they dare to call the full moon dirty because it has smudged its face with ink?

For every little trifle they blame you, my child. They are ready to find fault for nothing.

You tore your clothes while playing——is that why they call you untidy?

O, fie! What would they call an autumn morning that smiles through its ragged clouds?

Take no heed of what they say to you, my child.

They make a long list of your misdeeds.

Everybody knows how you love sweet things——is that why they call you greedy?

O, fie! What then would they call us who love you?

责备

为什么你眼里有了眼泪，我的孩子？

他们真是可怕，常常无谓地责备你！

你写字时墨水玷污了你的手和脸——这就是他们所以骂你龌龊的缘故么？

呵，呸！他们也敢因为圆圆的月儿用墨水涂了脸，便骂它龌龊么？

他们总要为了每一件小事去责备你，我的孩子。他们总是无谓地寻人错处。

你游戏时扯破了衣服——这就是他们说你不整洁的缘故？

呵，呸！秋之晨从它的破碎的云衣中露出微笑，那么，他们要叫它什么呢？

他们对你说什么话，尽管可以不去理睬他，我的孩子。

他们把你做错的事长长地记了一笔账。

谁都知道你是十分喜欢糖果的——这就是他们所以称你作贪婪的缘故么？

呵，呸！我们是喜欢你的，那么他们要叫我们什么呢？

THE JUDGE

Say of him what you please, but I know my child's failings.

I do not love him because he is good, but because he is my little child.

How should you know how dear he can be when you try to weigh his merits against his faults?

When I must punish him he becomes all the more a part of my being.

When I cause his tears to come my heart weeps with him.

I alone have a right to blame and punish, for he only may chastise who loves.

审判官

你想说他什么尽管说罢，但是我知道我孩子的短处。

我爱他并不因为他好，只是因为他是我的小小的孩子。

你如果把他的好处与坏处两两相权，你怎会知道他是如何地可爱呢？

当我必须责罚他的时候，他更成为我生命的一部分了。

当我使他的眼泪流出时，我的心也和他同哭了。

只有我才有权去骂他，去责备他；因为只有热爱人的人才可以惩戒人。

PLAYTHINGS

Child, how happy you are sitting in the dust, playing with a broken twig all the morning.

I smile at your play with that little bit of a broken twig.

I am busy with my accounts, adding up figures by the hour.

Perhaps you glance at me and think, "What a stupid game to spoil your morning with!"

Child, I have forgotten the art of being absorbed in sticks and mud—pies.

I seek out costly playthings, and gather lumps of gold and silver.

With whatever you find you create your glad games, I spent both my time and my strength over things I never can obtain.

In my frail canoe I struggle to cross the sea of desire, and forget that I too am playing a game.

玩具

孩子，你真是快活呀！一早晨坐在泥土里，耍着折下来的小树枝儿。

我微笑着看你在那里耍弄那根折下来的小树枝儿。

我正忙着算账，一小时一小时在那里加叠数字。

也许你在看我，心想："这种好没趣的游戏，竟把你一早晨的好时间浪费掉了！"

孩子，我忘了聚精会神玩耍树枝与泥饼的方法了。

我寻求贵重的玩具，收集金块与银块。

你呢，无论找到什么便去做你的快乐的游戏；我呢，却把我的时间与力气都浪费在那些我永不能得到的东西上。

我在我的脆薄的独木船里挣扎着，要航过欲望之海，竟忘了我也是在那里做游戏了。

THE ASTRONOMER

~✆~

I only said, "When in the evening the round full moon gets entangled among the branches of that Kadam tree, couldn't somebody catch it?"

But dada[①] laughed at me and said, "Baby, you are the silliest child I have ever known. The moon is ever so far from us, how could anybody catch it?"

I said, "Dada, how foolish you are! When mother looks out of her window and smiles down at us playing, would you call her far away?"

Still dada said, "You are a stupid child! But, baby, where could you find a net big enough to catch the moon with?"

I said, "Surely you could catch it with your hands."

But dada laughed and said, "You are the silliest child I have known. If it came nearer, you would see how big the moon is."

I said, "Dada, what nonsense they teach at your school! When mother bends her face down to kiss us does her face look very big?"

But still dada says, "You are a stupid child."

---

① Elder brother.

天文家

我不过说："当傍晚圆圆的满月挂在迦昙波 ① 的枝头时，有人能去捉住它么？"

哥哥却对我笑道："孩子呀，你真是我所见到的顶顶傻的孩子。月亮离我们这样远，谁能去捉住它呢？"

我说："哥哥，你真傻！当妈妈向窗外探望，微笑着往下看我们游戏时，你也能说她远么？"

哥哥还是说："你这个傻孩子！但是，孩子，你到哪里去找一个大得能逮住月亮的网呢？"

我说："你自然可以用双手去捉住它呀。"

但哥哥还是笑着说："你真是我所见到的顶顶傻的孩子！如果月亮走近了，你便知道它是多么大了。"

我说："哥哥，你们学校里所教的，真是没有用呀！当妈妈低下脸儿跟我们亲嘴时，她的脸看来也是很大的么？"

但哥哥还是说："你真是一个傻孩子。"

---

① 意译"白花"，即昙花。

CLOUDS AND WAVES

Mother, the folk who live up in the clouds call out to me——

"We play from the time we wake till the day ends.

"We play with the golden dawn, we play with the silver moon."

I ask, "But, how am I to get up to you?"

They answer, "Come to the edge of the earth, lift up your hands to the sky, and you will be taken up into the clouds."

"My mother is waiting for me at home," I say, "How can I leave her and come?"

Then they smile and float away.

But I know a nicer game than that, mother.

I shall be the cloud and you the moon.

I shall cover you with both my hands, and our house-top will be the blue sky.

The folk who live in the waves call out to me——

"We sing from morning till night; on and on we travel and know not where we pass."

I ask, "But, how am I to join you?"

They tell me, "Come to the edge of the shore and stand with your eyes tight shut, and you will be carried out upon the waves."

I say, "My mother always wants me at home in the evening——how can I leave her and go?"

Then they smile, dance and pass by.

But I know a better game than that.

I will be the waves and you will be a strange shore.

I shall roll on and on and on, and break upon your lap with laughter.

And no one in the world will know where we both are.

云与波

ᘓᘏᘓᘏ

妈妈，住在云端的人对我唤道——

"我们从醒的时候游戏到白日终止。

"我们与黄金色的曙光游戏，我们与银白色的月亮游戏。"

我问道："但是，我怎么能够上你那里去呢？"

他们答道："你到地球的边上来，举手向天，就可以被接到云端里来了。"

"我妈妈在家里等我呢，"我说，"我怎么能离开她而来呢？"

于是他们微笑着浮游而去。

但是我知道一件比这更好的游戏，妈妈。

我做云，你做月亮。

我用两只手遮盖你，我们的屋顶就是青碧的天空。

住在波浪上的人对我唤道——

"我们从早晨唱歌到晚上；我们前进又前进地旅行，也不知我们所经过的是什么地方。"

我问道："但是，我怎么才能加入你们的队伍呢？"

他们告诉我说："来到岸旁，站在那里，紧闭你的两眼，你就被带到波浪上来了。"

我说："傍晚的时候，我妈妈常要我在家里——我怎么能离开她而去呢？"

于是他们微笑着，跳着舞奔流过去。

但是我知道一件比这更好的游戏。

我是波浪，你是陌生的岸。

我奔流而进，进，进，笑哈哈地撞碎在你的膝上。

世界上就没有一个人会知道我们俩在什么地方。

THE CHAMPA FLOWER

Supposing I became a champa flower, just for fun, and grew on a branch high up that tree, and shook in the wind with laughter and danced upon the newly budded leaves, would you know me, mother?

You would call, "Baby, where are you?" and I should laugh to myself and keep quite quiet.

I should slyly open my petals and watch you at your work.

When after your bath, with wet hair spread on your shoulders, you walked through the shadow of the champa tree to the little court where you say your prayers, you would notice the scent of the flower, but not know that it came from me.

When after the midday meal you sat at the window reading Ramayana, and the tree's shadow fell over your hair and your lap, I should fling my wee little shadow on to the page of your book, just where you were reading.

But would you guess that it was the tiny shadow of your little child?

When in the evening you went to the cowshed with the lighted lamp in your hand, I should suddenly drop on to the earth again and be your own baby once more, and beg you to tell me a story.

"Where have you been, you naughty child?"

"I won't tell you, mother." That's what you and I would say then.

金色花

假如我变了一朵金色花[①]，为了好玩，长在树的高枝上，笑嘻嘻地在空中摇摆，又在新叶上跳舞，妈妈，你会认识我么？

你要是叫道："孩子，你在哪里呀？"我暗暗地在那里匿笑，却一声儿不响。

我要悄悄地开放花瓣儿，看着你工作。

当你沐浴后，湿发披在两肩，穿过金色花的林荫，走到做祷告的小庭院时，你会嗅到这花香，却不知道这香气是从我身上来的。

当你吃过午饭，坐在窗前读《罗摩衍那》[②]，那棵树的阴影落在你的头发与膝上时，我便要将我小小的影子投在你的书页上，正投在你所读的地方。

但是你会猜得出这就是你孩子的小小影子么？

当你黄昏时拿了灯到牛棚里去，我便要突然地再落到地上来，又成了你的孩子，求你讲故事给我听。

"你到哪里去了，你这坏孩子？"

"我不告诉你，妈妈。"这就是你同我那时所要说的话了。

---

① 印度圣树，木兰花属植物，开金黄色碎花。译名亦作"瞻波伽"或"占波"。

② 印度的一部叙事诗，相传系第五世纪 Valmiki 所作。全诗二万四千章，分为七卷。

FAIRYLAND

If people came to know where my king's palace is, it would vanish into the air.

The walls are of white silver and the roof of shining gold.

The queen lives in a palace with seven courtyards, and she wears a jewel that cost all the wealth of seven kingdoms.

But, let me tell you, mother, in a whisper, where my king's palace is.

It is at the corner of our terrace where the pot of the tulsi plant stands.

The princess lies sleeping on the faraway shore of the seven impassable seas.

There is none in the world who can find her but myself.

She has bracelets on her arms and pearl drops in her ears; her hair sweeps down upon the floor.

She will wake when I touch her with my magic wand, and jewels will fall from her lips when she smiles.

But let me whisper in your ear, mother; she is there in the corner of our terrace where the pot of the tulsi plant stands.

When it is time for you to go to the river for your bath, step up to that terrace on the roof.

I sit on the corner where the shadows of the walls meet

together.

Only puss is allowed to come with me, for she knows where the barber in the story lives.

But let me whisper, mother, in your ear where the barber in the story lives.

It is at the corner of the terrace where the pot of the tulsi plant stands.

仙人世界

如果人们知道了我的国王的宫殿在哪里，它就会消失在空气中的。

墙壁是白色的银，屋顶是耀眼的黄金。

皇后住在有七个庭院的宫苑里；她戴的一串珠宝，值得整整七个王国的全部财富。

不过，让我悄悄地告诉你，妈妈，我的国王的宫殿究竟在哪里。

它就在我们阳台的角上，在那栽着杜尔茜花的花盆放着的地方。

公主躺在远远的、隔着七个不可逾越的重洋的那一岸沉睡着。

除了我自己，世界上便没有人能够找到她。

她臂上有镯子，她耳上挂着珍珠，她的头发拖到地板上。

当我用我的魔杖点触她的时候，她就会醒过来；而当她微笑时，珠玉将会从她唇边落下来。

不过，让我在你的耳朵边悄悄地告诉你，妈妈，她就住在我们阳台的角上，在那栽着杜尔茜花的花盆放着的地方。

当你要到河里洗澡的时候，你走上屋顶的那座阳台来罢。

我就坐在墙的阴影所聚会的一个角落里。

我只让小猫儿跟我在一起，因为它知道那故事里的理发匠到底住在哪里。

他住的地方，就在阳台的角上，在那栽着杜尔茜花的花盆放着的地方。

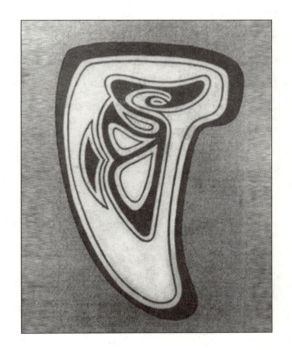

THE LAND OF THE EXILE

∾ၥⱱ∾

Mother, the light has grown grey in the sky; I do not know what the time is.

There is no fun in my play, so I have come to you. It is Saturday, our holiday.

Leave off your work, mother; sit here by the window and tell me where the desert of Tepantar in the fairy tale is?

The shadow of the rains has covered the day from end to end.

The fierce lightning is scratching the sky with its nails.

When the clouds rumble and it thunders, I love to be afraid in my heart and cling to you.

When the heavy rain patters for hours on the bamboo leaves, and our windows shake and rattle at the gusts of wind, I like to sit alone in the room, mother, with you, and hear you talk about the desert of Tepantar in the fairy tale.

Where is it, mother, on the shore of what sea, at the foot of what hills, in the kingdom of what king?

There are no hedges there to mark the fields, no footpath across it by which the villagers reach their village in the evening, or the woman who gathers dry sticks in the forest can bring her load to the market. With patches of yellow grass in the sand and only one tree where the pair of wise old birds have their nest, lies the desert of Tepantar.

I can imagine how, on just such a cloudy day, the young son of the king is riding alone on a grey horse through the desert, in search of the princess who lies imprisoned in the giant's palace across that unknown water.

When the haze of the rain comes down in the distant sky, and lightning starts up like a sudden fit of pain, does he remember his unhappy mother, abandoned by the king, sweeping the cow—stall and wiping her eyes, while he rides through the desert of Tepantar in the fairy tale?

See, mother, it is almost dark before the day is over, and there are no travellers yonder on the village road.

The shepherd boy has gone home early from the pasture, and men have left their fields to sit on mats under the eaves of their huts, watching the scowling clouds.

Mother, I have left all my books on the shelf—do not ask me to do my lessons now.

When I grow up and am big like my father, I shall learn all that must be learnt.

But just for to—day, tell me, mother, where the desert of Tepantar in the fairy tale is?

流放的地方

妈妈，天空上的光成了灰色了；我不知道是什么时候了。

我玩得怪没劲儿的，所以到你这里来了。这是星期六，是我们的休息日。

放下你的活计，妈妈，坐在靠窗的一边，告诉我童话里的特潘塔沙漠在什么地方。

雨的影子遮掩了整个白天。

凶猛的电光用它的爪子抓着天空。

当乌云在轰轰地响着，天打着雷的时候，我总爱心里带着恐惧爬伏到你的身上。

当大雨倾泻在竹叶子上好几个钟头，而我们的窗户为狂风震得咯咯发响的时候，我就爱独自和你坐在屋里，妈妈，听你讲童话里的特潘塔沙漠的故事。

它在哪里，妈妈？在哪一个海洋的岸上？在哪些个山峰的脚下？在哪一个国王的国土里？

田地上没有此疆彼壤的界石，也没有村人在黄昏时走回家的或妇人在树林里捡拾枯枝而捆载到市场上去的道路。沙地上只有一小块一小块的黄色草地，只有一株树，就是那一对聪明的老鸟儿在那里做窝的，那个地方就是特潘塔沙漠。

我能够想象得到，就在这样一个乌云密布的日子，国王的年轻的儿子，怎样独自骑着一匹灰色马，走过这个沙漠，去寻找那被囚禁在不可知的重洋之外的巨人宫里的公主。

当雨雾在遥远的天空下降，电光像一阵突然发作的痛楚的痉挛似的闪射的时候，他可记得他的不幸的母亲，为国王所弃，正在打扫牛棚，眼里流着眼泪，当他骑马走过童话里的特潘塔沙漠的时候？

看，妈妈，一天还没有完，天色就差不多黑了，那边村庄的路上没有什么旅客了。

牧童早就从牧场上回家了，人们都已从田地里回来，坐在他们草屋檐下的草席上，眼望着阴沉的云块。

妈妈，我把我所有的书本都放在书架上了——不要叫我现在做功课。

当我长大了，大得像爸爸一样的时候，我将会学到必须学到的东西的。

但是，今天你可得告诉我，妈妈，童话里的特潘塔沙漠在什么地方。

THE RAINY DAY

Sullen clouds are gathering fast over the black fringe of the forest.

O, child, do not go out!

The palm trees in a row by the lake are smiting their heads against the dismal sky; the crows with their draggled wings are silent on the tamarind branches, and the eastern bank of the river is haunted by a deepening gloom.

Our cow is lowing loud, tied at the fence.

O, child, wait here till I bring her into the stall.

Men have crowded into the flooded field to catch the fishes as they escape from the over−flowing ponds; the rain water is running in rills through the narrow lanes like a laughing boy who has run away from his mother to tease her.

Listen, someone is shouting for the boatman at the ford.

O, child, the daylight is dim, and the crossing at the ferry is closed.

The sky seems to ride fast upon the madly−rushing rain; the water in the river is loud and impatient; women have hastened home early from the Ganges with their filled pitchers.

The evening lamps must be made ready.

O, child, do not go out!

The road to the market is desolate, the lane to the river is slippery. The wind is roaring and struggling among the bamboo branches like a wild beast tangled in a net.

雨天

乌云很快地集拢在森林的黝黑的边缘上。

孩子，不要出去呀！

湖边的一行棕树，向冥暗的天空撞着头；羽毛凌乱的乌鸦，静悄悄地栖在罗望子树的枝上。河的东岸正被乌沉沉的冥色所侵袭。

我们的牛系在篱上，高声鸣叫。

孩子，在这里等着，等我先把牛牵进牛棚里去。

许多人都挤在池水泛溢的田间，捉那从泛溢的池中逃出来的鱼儿。雨水成了小河，流过狭弄，好像一个嬉笑的孩子从他妈妈那里跑开，故意要恼她一样。

听呀，有人在浅滩上喊船夫呢。

孩子，天色冥暗了，渡头的摆渡已经停了。

　　天空好像是在滂沱的雨上快跑着；河里的水喧叫而且暴躁；妇人们早已拿着汲满了水的水罐，从恒河畔匆匆地回家了。

　　夜里用的灯，一定要预备好。

　　孩子，不要出去呀！

　　到市场去的大道已没有人走，到河边去的小路又很滑。风在竹林里咆哮着，挣扎着，好像一只落在网中的野兽。

PAPER BOATS

Day by day I float my paper boats one by one down the running stream.

In big black letters I write my name on them and the name of the village where I live.

I hope that someone in some strange land will find them and know who I am.

I load my little boats with shiuli flowers from our garden, and hope that these blooms of the dawn will be carried safely to land in the night.

I launch my paper boats and look up into the sky and see the little clouds setting their white bulging sails.

I know not what playmate of mine in the sky sends them down the air to race with my boats!

When night comes I bury my face in my arms and dream that my paper boats float on and on under the midnight stars.

The fairies of sleep are sailing in them, and the lading is their baskets full of dreams.

纸船

我每天把纸船一个个放在急流的溪中。

我用大黑字把我的名字和我住的村名写在纸船上。

我希望住在异地的人会得到这纸船,知道我是谁。

我把园中长的秀利花载在我的小船上,希望这些黎明开的花能在夜里被平平安安地带到岸上。

我把我的纸船投到水里,仰望天空,看见小朵的云正张着满鼓着风的白帆。

我不知道天上有我的什么游伴把这些船放下来同我的船比赛!

夜来了,我的脸埋在手臂里,梦见我的纸船在子夜的星光下缓缓地浮泛向前。

睡仙坐在船里,带着满载着梦的篮子。

THE SAILOR

The boat of the boatman Madhu is moored at the wharf of Rajgunj.

It is uselessly laden with jute, and has been lying there idle for ever so long.

If he would only lend me his boat, I should man her with a hundred oars, and hoist sails, five or six or seven.

I should never steer her to stupid markets.

I should sail the seven seas and the thirteen rivers of fairyland.

But, mother, you won't weep for me in a corner.

I am not going into the forest like Ramachandra to come back only after fourteen years.

I shall become the prince of the story, and fill my boat with whatever I like.

I shall take my friend Ashu with me. We shall sail merrily across the seven seas and the thirteen rivers of fairyland.

We shall set sail in the early morning light.

When at noontide you are bathing at the pond, we shall be in the land of a strange king.

We shall pass the ford of Tirpurni, and leave behind us the desert of Tepantar.

When we come back it will be getting dark, and I shall tell you of all that we have seen.

I shall cross the seven seas and the thirteen rivers of fairyland.

水手

船夫曼特胡的船只停泊在拉琪根琪码头。

这只船无用地装载着黄麻，无所事事地停泊在那里已经好久了。

只要他肯把他的船借给我，我就给它安装一百只桨，扬起五个或六个或七个布帆来。

我决不把它驾驶到愚蠢的市场上去。

我将航行遍仙人世界里的七个大海和十三条河道。

但是，妈妈，你不会躲在角落里为我哭泣。

我不会像罗摩犍陀罗①似的，到森林中去，一去十四年才回来。

我将成为故事中的王子，把我的船装满了我所喜欢的东西。

我将带我的朋友阿细和我做伴。我们要快快乐乐地航行于仙人世

---

① 即罗摩。他是印度叙事诗《罗摩衍那》中的主角。为了尊重父亲的诺言和维持弟兄间的友爱，他抛弃了继承王位的权利，和妻子悉多在森林中被放逐了十四年。

界里的七个大海和十三条河道。

我将在绝早的晨光里张帆航行。

中午，你正在池塘里洗澡的时候，我们将在一个陌生的国王的国土上了。

我们将经过特浦尼浅滩，把特潘塔沙漠抛落在我们的后边。

当我们回来的时候，天色快黑了，我将告诉你我们所见到的一切。

我将越过仙人世界里的七个大海和十三条河道。

THE FURTHER BANK

I long to go over there to the further bank of the river,

Where those boats are tied to the bamboo poles in a line;

Where men cross over in their boats in the morning with ploughs on their shoulders to till their far-away fields;

Where the cowherds make their lowing cattle swim across to the riverside pasture;

Whence they all come back home in the evening, leaving the jackals to howl in the island overgrown with weeds.

Mother, if you don't mind, I should like to become the boatman of the ferry when I am grown up.

They say there are strange pools hidden behind that high bank,

Where flocks of wild ducks come when the rains are over, and thick reeds grow round the margins where waterbirds lay their eggs;

Where snipes with their dancing tails stamp their tiny footprints upon the clean soft mud;

Where in the evening the tall grasses crested with white flowers invite the moonbeam to float upon their waves.

Mother, if you don't mind, I should like to become the boatman of the ferryboat when I am grown up.

I shall cross and cross back from bank to bank, and all the boys and girls of the village will wonder at me while they are bathing.

When the sun climbs the mid sky and morning wears on to noon, I shall come running to you, saying, "Mother, I am hungry!"

When the day is done and the shadows cower under the trees, I shall come back in the dusk.

I shall never go away from you into the town to work like father.

Mother, if you don't mind, I should like to become the boatman of the ferryboat when I am grown up.

对岸

我渴想到河的对岸去，

在那边，好些船只一行儿系在竹竿上；

人们在早晨乘船渡过那边去，肩上扛着犁头，去耕耘他们的远处的田；

在那边，牧人使他们鸣叫着的牛游泳到河旁的牧场去；

黄昏的时候，他们都回家了，只留下豺狼在这满长着野草的岛上哀叫。

妈妈，如果你不在意，我长大的时候，要做这渡船的船夫。

据说有好些古怪的池塘藏在这个高岸之后。

雨过去了，一群一群的野鹜飞到那里去。茂盛的芦苇在岸边四围生长，水鸟在那里生蛋；

竹鸡带着跳舞的尾巴，将它们细小的足印印在洁净的软泥上；

黄昏的时候，长草顶着白花，邀月光在长草的波浪上浮游。

妈妈，如果你不在意，我长大的时候，要做这渡船的船夫。

我要自此岸至彼岸，渡过来，渡过去，所有村中正在那儿沐浴的男孩女孩，都要诧异地望着我。

太阳升到中天，早晨变为正午了，我将跑到你那里去，说道："妈妈，我饿了！"

一天完了，影子俯伏在树底下，我便要在黄昏中回家来。

我将永不像爸爸那样，离开你到城里去做事。

妈妈，如果你不在意，我长大的时候，要做这渡船的船夫。

THE FLOWER-SCHOOL

When storm clouds rumble in the sky and June showers come down,

The moist east wind comes marching over the heath to blow its bagpipes among the bamboos.

Then crowds of flowers come out of a sudden, from nobody knows where, and dance upon the grass in wild glee.

Mother, I really think the flowers go to school underground.

They do their lessons with doors shut, and if they want to come out to play before it is time, their master makes them stand in a corner.

When the rains come they have their holidays.

Branches clash together in the forest, and the leaves rustle in the wild wind, the thunder-clouds clap their giant hands and the flower children rush out in dresses of pink and yellow and white.

Do you know, mother, their home is in the sky, where the stars are.

Haven't you seen how eager they are to get there? Don't you know why they are in such a hurry?

Of course, I can guess to whom they raise their arms: they have their mother as I have my own.

花的学校

当雷云在天上轰响，六月的阵雨落下的时候，

湿润的东风走过荒野，在竹林中吹着口笛。

于是一群一群的花从无人知道的地方突然跑出来，在绿草上狂欢地跳着舞。

妈妈，我真的觉得那群花朵是在地下的学校里上学。

它们关了门做功课。如果它们想在散学以前出来游戏，它们的老师是要罚它们站壁角的。

雨一来，它们便放假了。

树枝在林中互相碰触着，绿叶在狂风里萧萧地响，雷云拍着大手。这时花孩子们便穿了紫的、黄的、白的衣裳，冲了出来。

你可知道，妈妈，它们的家是在天上，在星星所住的地方。

你没有看见它们怎样地急着要到那儿去么？你不知道它们为什么那样急急忙忙么？

我自然能够猜得出它们是对谁扬起双臂来：它们也有它们的妈妈，就像我有我自己的妈妈一样。

THE MERCHANT

Imagine, mother, that you are to stay at home and I am to travel into strange lands.

Imagine that my boat is ready at the landing fully laden.

Now think well, mother, before you say what I shall bring for you when I come back.

Mother, do you want heaps and heaps of gold?

There, by the banks of golden streams, fields are full of golden harvest.

And in the shade of the forest path the golden champa flowers drop on the ground.

I will gather them all for you in many hundred baskets.

Mother, do you want pearls big as the rain-drops of autumn?

I shall cross to the pearl island shore.

There in the early morning light pearls tremble on the meadow flowers, pearls drop on the grass, and pearls are scattered on the sand in spray by the wild sea-waves.

My brother shall have a pair of horses with wings to fly among the clouds.

For father I shall bring a magic pen that, without his knowing, will write of itself.

For you, mother, I must have the casket and jewel that cost seven kings their kingdoms.

商人

妈妈，让我们想象，你待在家里，我到异邦去旅行。

再想象，我的船已经装得满满的，在码头上等候启碇了。

现在，妈妈，你想一想告诉我，回来时我要带些什么给你。

妈妈，你要一堆一堆的黄金么？

在金河的两岸，田野里全是金色的稻实。

在林荫的路上，金色花也一朵一朵地落在地上。

我要为你把它们全都收拾起来，放在好几百个篮子里。

妈妈，你要秋天的雨点一般大的珍珠么？

我要渡海到珍珠岛的岸上去。

那个地方，在清晨的曙光里，珠子在草地的野花上颤动，珠子落在绿草上，珠子被汹狂的海浪一大把一大把地撒在沙滩上。

我的哥哥呢，我要送他一对有翼的马，会在云端飞翔的。

爸爸呢，我要带一支有魔力的笔给他，他还没有感觉到，笔就写出字来了。

你呢，妈妈，我要把值七个王国的首饰箱和珠宝送给你。

SYMPATHY

If I were only a little puppy, not your baby, mother dear, would you say "No" to me if I tried to eat from your dish?

Would you drive me off, saying to me, "Get away, you naughty little puppy?"

Then go, mother, go! I will never come to you when you call me, and never let you feed me any more.

If I were only a little green parrot, and not your baby, mother dear, would you keep me chained lest I should fly away?

Would you shake your finger at me and say, "What an ungrateful wretch of a bird! It is gnawing at its chain day and night?"

Then, go, mother, go! I will run away into the woods; I will never let you take me in your arms again.

同情

如果我只是一只小狗，而不是你的小孩，亲爱的妈妈，当我想吃你盘里的东西时，你要向我说"不"么？

你要赶开我，对我说道："滚开，你这淘气的小狗"么？

那么，走罢，妈妈，走罢！当你叫唤我的时候，我就永不到你那里去，也永不要你再喂我吃东西了。

如果我只是一只绿色的小鹦鹉，而不是你的小孩，亲爱的妈妈，你要把我紧紧地锁住，怕我飞走么？

你要对我指指点点地说道："怎样的一只不知感恩的贱鸟呀！整日整夜地尽在咬它的链子"么？

那么，走罢，妈妈，走罢！我要跑到树林里去；我就永不再让你将我抱在你的臂里了。

VOCATION

೧ಲಲೂ

When the gong sounds ten in the morning and I walk to school by our lane,

Everyday I meet the hawker crying, "Bangles, crystal bangles!"

There is nothing to hurry him on, there is no road he must take, no place he must go to, no time when he must come home.

I wish I were a hawker, spending my day in the road, crying, "Bangles, crystal bangles!"

When at four in the afternoon I come back from the school,

I can see through the gate of that house the gardener digging the ground.

He does what he likes with his spade, he soils his clothes with dust, nobody takes him to task if he gets baked in the sun or gets wet.

I wish I were a gardener digging away at the garden with nobody to stop me from digging.

Just as it gets dark in the evening and my mother sends me to bed,

I can see through my open window the watchman walking up and down.

The lane is dark and lonely and the street—lamp stands like a giant with one red eye in its head.

The watchman swings his lantern and walks with his shadow at his side, and never once goes to bed in his life.

I wish I were a watchman walking the streets all night, chasing the shadows with my lantern.

职业

早晨，钟敲十下的时候，我沿着我们的小巷到学校去。

每天我都遇见那个小贩，他叫道："镯子呀，亮晶晶的镯子！"

他没有什么事情急着要做，他没有哪条街道一定要走，他没有什么地方一定要去，他没有什么规定的时间一定要回家。

我愿意我是一个小贩，在街上过日子，叫着："镯子呀，亮晶晶的镯子！"

下午四点钟，我从学校里回家。

从一家门口，我看见一个园丁在那里掘地。

他用他的锄子，要怎么掘，便怎么掘，他被尘土污了衣裳。如果他被太阳晒黑了或是身上被打湿了，都没有人骂他。

我愿意我是一个园丁，在花园里掘地，谁也不来阻止我。

天色刚黑，妈妈就送我上床。

从开着的窗口，我看见更夫走来走去。

小巷又黑又冷清，路灯立在那里，像一个头上生着一只红眼睛的巨人。

更夫摇着他的提灯，跟他身边的影子一起走着，他一生一次都没有上床去过。

我愿意我是一个更夫，整夜在街上走，提了灯去追逐影子。

SUPERIOR

Mother, your baby is silly! She is so absurdly childish!

She does not know the difference between the lights in the streets and the stars.

When we play at eating with pebbles, she thinks they are real food, and tries to put them into her mouth.

When I open a book before her and ask her to learn her a, b, c, she tears the leaves with her hands and roars for joy at nothing; this is your baby's way of doing her lesson.

When I shake my head at her in anger and scold her and call her naughty, she laughs and thinks it great fun.

Everybody knows that father is away, but, if in play I call aloud "Father", she looks about her in excitement and thinks that father is near.

When I hold my class with the donkeys that our washerman brings to carry away the clothes and I warn her that I am the school-master, she will scream for no reason and call me dādā.

Your baby wants to catch the moon. She is so funny; she calls Ganesh Gānush.

Mother, your baby is silly, she is so absurdly childish!

长者

妈妈，你的孩子真傻！她是那么可笑地不懂事！
她不知道路灯和星星的区别。
当我们玩着把小石子当食物的游戏时，她便以为它们真是吃的东西，竟想放进嘴里去。

当我翻开一本书，放在她面前，要她读 a，b，c 时，她却用手把书页撕了，无端快活地叫起来；你的孩子就是这样做功课的。

当我生气地对她摇头，骂她，说她顽皮时，她却哈哈大笑，以为很有趣。

谁都知道爸爸不在家。但是，如果我在游戏时高叫一声"爸爸"，她便要高兴地四面张望，以为爸爸真是近在身边。

当我把洗衣人带来的运载衣服回去的驴子当做学生，并且警告她说，我是老师时，她却无缘无故地乱叫起我哥哥来。

你的孩子要捉月亮。她是这样的可笑；她把格尼许[①]唤作琪奴许。

妈妈，你的孩子真傻，她是那么可笑地不懂事！

~~~~~~~~~~

THE LITTLE BIG MAN

I am small because I am a little child. I shall be big when I am

---

① 是印度的一个普通名字，也是象头神之名。

as old as my father is.

My teacher will come and say, "It is late, bring your slate and your books."

I shall tell him, "Do you not know I am as big as father? And I must not have lessons any more."

My master will wonder and say, "He can leave his books if he likes, for he is grown up."

I shall dress myself and walk to the fair where the crowd is thick.

My uncle will come rushing up to me and say, "You will get lost, my boy; let me carry you."

I shall answer, "Can't you see, uncle, I am as big as father? I must go to the fair alone."

Uncle will say, "Yes, he can go wherever he likes, for he is grown up."

Mother will come from her bath when I am giving money to my nurse, for I shall know how to open the box with my key.

Mother will say, "What are you about, naughty child?"

I shall tell her, "Mother, don't you know, I am as big as father, and I must give silver to my nurse."

Mother will say to herself, "He can give money to whom he likes, for he is grown up."

In the holiday time in October father will come home and, thinking that I am still a baby, will bring for me from the town little shoes and small silken frocks.

I shall say, "Father, give them to my dādā, for I am as big as you are."

Father will think and say, "He can buy his own clothes if he likes, for he is grown up."

小大人

我人很小，因为我是一个小孩子。到了我像爸爸一样年纪时，便要变大了。

我的先生要是走来说道："时候晚了，把你的石板、你的书拿来。"

我便要告诉他道："你不知道我已经同爸爸一样大了么？我决不再学什么功课了。"

我的老师便将惊异地说道："他读书不读书可以随便，因为他是大人了。"

我将自己穿了衣裳，走到人群拥挤的市场里去。

我的叔叔要是跑过来说道："你要迷路了，我的孩子，让我抱着你罢。"

我便要回答道："你没有看见么，叔叔？我已经同爸爸一样大了。我决定要独自一人到市场里去。"

叔叔便将说道："是的，他随便到哪里去都可以，因为他是大人了。"

当我正拿钱给我保姆时，妈妈便要从浴室中出来，因为我是知道怎样用我的钥匙去开银箱的。

妈妈要是说道："你在做什么呀，顽皮的孩子？"

我便要告诉她道："妈妈，你不知道我已经同爸爸一样大了么？我必须拿钱给保姆。"

妈妈便将自言自语道："他可以随便把钱给他所喜欢的人，因为他是大人了。"

当十月里放假的时候，爸爸将要回家。他会以为我还是一个小孩子，为我从城里带了小鞋子和小绸衫来。

我便要说道："爸爸，把这些东西给哥哥罢，因为我已经同你一样大了。"

爸爸便将想一想，说道："他可以随便去买他自己穿的衣裳，因为他是大人了。"

TWELVE OCLOCK

Mother, I do want to leave off my lessons now. I have been at my book all the morning.

You say it is only twelve o'clock. Suppose it isn't any later; can't you ever think it is afternoon when it is only twelve o'clock?

I can easily imagine now that the sun has reached the edge of that rice—field, and the old fisher—woman is gathering herbs for her supper by the side of the pond.

I can just shut my eyes and think that the shadows are growing darker under the madar tree, and the water in the pond looks shiny black.

If twelve o'clock can come in the night, why can't the night come when it is twelve o'clock?

十二点钟

妈妈，我真想现在不做功课了。我整个早晨都在念书呢。

你说，现在还不过是十二点钟。假定不会晚过十二点罢；难道你不能把不过是十二点钟想象成下午么？

我能够很容易地想象：现在太阳已经到了那片稻田的边缘上了，老态龙钟的渔婆正在池边采撷香草做她的晚餐。

我闭上了眼就能够想到，马塔尔树下的阴影是更深黑了，池塘里的水看来黑得发亮。

假如十二点钟能够在黑夜里来到，为什么黑夜不能在十二点钟的时候来到呢？

AUTHORSHIP

∽๑∾

You say that father writes a lot of books, but what he writes I don't understand.

He was reading to you all the evening, but could you really make out what he meant?

What nice stories, mother, you can tell us! Why can't father write like that, I wonder?

Did he never hear from his own mother stories of giants and fairies and princesses?

Has he forgotten them all?

Often when he gets late for his bath you have to go and call him an hundred times.

You wait and keep his dishes warm for him, but he goes on writing and forgets.

Father always plays at making books.

If ever I go to play in father's room, you come and call me, "What a naughty child!"

If I make the slightest noise, you say, "Don't you see that father's at his work?"

What's the fun of always writing and writing?

When I take up father's pen or pencil and write upon his book just as he does,—a, b, c, d, e, f, g, h, i,—why do you get cross with me, then, mother?

You never say a word when father writes.

When my father wastes such heaps of paper, mother, you don't seem to mind at all.

But if I take only one sheet to make a boat with, you say, "Child, how troublesome you are!"

What do you think of father's spoiling sheets and sheets of paper with black marks all over on both sides?

著作家

你说爸爸写了许多书，但我却不懂得他所写的东西。

他整个黄昏读书给你听，但是你真懂得他的意思么？

妈妈，你给我们讲的故事，真是好听呀！我很奇怪，爸爸为什么不能写那样的书呢？

难道他从来没有从他自己的妈妈那里听见过巨人、神仙和公主的故事么？

还是已经完全忘记了？

他常常耽误了沐浴，你不得不走去叫他一百多次。

你总要等候着，把他的菜温着等他。但他忘了，还尽管写下去。

爸爸老是以著书为游戏。

如果我一走进爸爸房里去游戏。你就要走来叫道："真是一个顽皮的孩子！"

如果我稍微弄出一点声音，你就要说："你没有看见你爸爸正在工作么？"

老是写了又写，有什么趣味呢？

当我拿起爸爸的钢笔或铅笔，像他一模一样地在他的书上写着，——a，b，c，d，e，f，g，h，i，——那时，你为什么跟我生气呢，妈妈？

爸爸写时，你却从来不说一句话。

当我爸爸耗费了那么一大堆纸时，妈妈，你似乎全不在乎。

但是，如果我只取了一张纸去做一只船，你却要说："孩子，你真讨厌！"

你对于爸爸拿黑点子涂满了纸的两面，污损了许多许多张纸，心里以为怎样呢？

THE WICKED POSTMAN

Why do you sit there on the floor so quiet and silent, tell me, mother dear?

The rain is coming in through the open window, making you all wet, and you don't mind it.

Do you hear the gong striking four? It is time for my brother to come home from school.

What has happened to you that you look so strange?

Haven't you got a letter from father today?

I saw the postman bringing letters in his bag for almost everybody in the town.

Only, father's letters he keeps to read himself. I am sure the postman is a wicked man.

But don't be unhappy about that, mother dear.

Tomorrow is market day in the next village. You ask your maid to buy some pens and papers.

I myself will write all father's letters; you will not find a single mistake.

I shall write from A right up to K.

But, mother, why do you smile?

You don't believe that I can write as nicely as father does!

But I shall rule my paper carefully, and write all the letters beautifully big.

When I finish my writing, do you think I shall be so foolish as father and drop it into the horrid postman's bag?

I shall bring it to you myself without waiting, and letter by letter help you to read my writing.

I know the postman does not like to give you the really nice letters.

恶邮差

你为什么坐在那边地板上不言不动的？告诉我呀，亲爱的妈妈。

雨从开着的窗口打进来了，把你身上全打湿了，你却不管。

你听见钟已打了四下么？正是哥哥从学校里回家的时候了。

到底发生了什么事，你的神色这样不对？

你今天没有接到爸爸的信么？

我看见邮差在他的袋里带了许多信来，几乎镇里的每个人都分送到了。

只有爸爸的信，他留起来给他自己看。我确信这个邮差是个坏人。

但是不要因此不乐呀，亲爱的妈妈。

明天是邻村市集的日子。你叫女仆去买些笔和纸来。

我自己会写爸爸所写的一切信；使你找不出一点错处来。

我要从 A 字一直写到 K 字。

但是，妈妈，你为什么笑呢？

你不相信我能写得像爸爸一样好？

但是我将用心画格子，把所有的字母都写得又大又美。

当我写好了时，你以为我也像爸爸那样傻，把它投入可怕的邮差的袋中么？

我立刻就自己送来给你，而且一个字母，一个字母地帮助你读。

我知道那邮差是不肯把真正的好信送给你的。

THE HERO

Mother, let us imagine we are travelling and passing through a strange and dangerous country.

You are riding in a palanquin and I am trotting by you on a red horse.

It is evening and the sun goes down. The waste of Joradighi lies wan and grey before us. The land is desolate and barren.

You are frightened and thinking — "I know not where we have come to."

I say to you, "Mother, do not be afraid."

The meadow is prickly with spiky grass, and through it runs a narrow broken path.

There are no cattle to be seen in the wide field; they have gone to their village stalls.

It grows dark and dim on the land and sky, and we cannot tell where we are going.

Suddenly you call me and ask me in a whisper, "What light is that near the bank?"

Just then there bursts out a fearful yell, and figures come running towards us.

You sit crouched in your palanquin and repeat the names of the gods in prayer.

The bearers, shaking in terror, hide themselves in the thorny bush.

I shout to you, "Don't be afraid, mother, I am here."

With long sticks in their hands and hair all wild about their heads, they come nearer and nearer.

I shout, "Have a care! You villains! One step more and you

are dead men."

They give another terrible yell and rush forward.

You clutch my hand and say, "Dear boy, for heaven's sake, keep away from them."

I say, "Mother, just you watch me."

Then I spur my horse for a wild gallop, and my sword and buckler clash against each other.

The fight becomes so fearful, mother, that it would give you a cold shudder could you see it from your palanquin.

Many of them fly, and a great number are cut to pieces.

I know you are thinking, sitting all by yourself, that your boy must be dead by this time.

But I come to you all stained with blood, and say, "Mother, the fight is over now."

You come out and kiss me, pressing me to your heart, and you say to yourself,

"I don't know what I should do if I hadn't my boy to escort me."

A thousand useless things happen day after day, and why couldn't such a thing come true by chance?

It would be like a story in a book.

My brother would say, "Is it possible? I always thought he was so delicate!"

Our village people would all say in amazement, "Was it not lucky that the boy was with his mother?"

英雄

妈妈，让我们想象我们正在旅行，经过一个陌生而危险的国土。

你坐在一顶轿子里，我骑着一匹红马，在你旁边跑着。

是黄昏的时候，太阳已经下山了。约拉地希的荒地疲乏而灰暗地展开在我们面前。大地是凄凉而荒芜的。

你害怕了，想道——"我不知道我们到了什么地方了。"

我对你说道："妈妈，不要害怕。"

草地上刺蓬蓬地长着针尖似的草，一条狭而崎岖的小道通过这块草地。

在这片广大的地面上看不见一只牛；它们已经回到它们村里的牛棚里去了。

天色黑了下来，大地和天空都显得朦朦胧胧的，而我们不能说出我们正走向什么所在。

突然间，你叫我，悄悄地问我道："靠近河岸的是什么火光呀？"

正在那个时候，一阵可怕的呐喊声爆发了，好些人影子向我们跑过来。

你蹲坐在你的轿子里，嘴里反复地祷念着神的名字。

轿夫们，怕得发抖，躲藏在荆棘丛中。

我向你喊道："不要害怕，妈妈，有我在这里。"

他们手里执着长棒，头发披散着，越走越近了。

我喊道："要当心！你们这些坏蛋！再向前走一步，你们就要送命了。"

他们又发出一阵可怕的呐喊声，向前冲过来。

你抓住我的手，说道："好孩子，看在上天面上，躲开他们罢。"

我说道："妈妈，你瞧我的。"

于是我刺策着我的马匹，猛奔过去，我的剑和盾彼此碰着作响。

这一场战斗是那么激烈，妈妈，如果你从轿子里看得见的话，你一定会发冷战的。

他们之中，许多人逃走了，还有好些人被砍杀了。

我知道你那时独自坐在那里，心里正在想着，你的孩子这时候一定已经死了。

但是我跑到你的跟前，浑身溅满了鲜血，说道："妈妈，现在战争已经结束了。"

你从轿子里走出来，吻着我，把我搂在你的心头，你自言自语地说道：

"如果没有我的孩子护送我，我简直不知道怎么办才好。"

一千件无聊的事天天在发生，为什么这样一件事不能够偶然实现呢？

这很像一本书里的一个故事。

我的哥哥要说道："这是可能的事么？我老是想，他是那么嫩弱呢！"

　　我们村里的人们都要惊讶地说道："这孩子正和他妈妈在一起，这不是很幸运么？"

THE END

It is time for me to go, mother; I am going.

When in the paling darkness of the lonely dawn you stretch out your arms for your baby in the bed, I shall say, "Baby is not there!" —mother, I am going.

I shall become a delicate draught of air and caress you; and I shall be ripples in the water when you bathe, and kiss you and kiss you again.

In the gusty night when the rain patters on the leaves you will hear my whisper in your bed, and my laughter will flash with the lightning through the open window into your room.

If you lie awake, thinking of your baby till late into the night, I shall sing to you from the stars, "Sleep, mother, sleep."

On the straying moonbeams I shall steal over your bed, and lie upon your bosom while you sleep.

I shall become a dream, and through the little opening of your eyelids I shall slip into the depths of your sleep, and when you wake up and look round startled, like a twinkling firefly I shall flit out into the darkness.

When, on the great festival of puja, the neighbours' children come and play about the house, I shall melt into the music of the flute and throb in your heart all day.

Dear auntie will come with puja-presents and will ask, "Where is our baby, sister?" Mother, you will tell her softly, "He is in the pupils of my eyes, he is in my body and in my soul."

告别

是我走的时候了，妈妈，我走了。

当清寂的黎明，你在暗中伸出双臂，要抱你睡在床上的孩子时，我要说道："孩子不在那里呀！"——妈妈，我走了。

我要变成一股清风抚摸着你；我要变成水中的涟漪，当你浴时，把你吻了又吻。

大风之夜，当雨点在树叶上淅沥时，你在床上会听见我的微语；当电光从开着的窗口闪进你的屋里时，我的笑声也偕了他一同闪进了。

如果你醒着躺在床上，想你的孩子直到深夜，我便要从星空向你唱道："睡呀！妈妈，睡呀。"

我要坐在各处游荡的月光上，偷偷地来到你的床上，乘你睡着时，躺在你的胸上。

我要变成一个梦儿，从你眼皮的微缝中钻到你的睡眠的深处。当你醒来吃惊地四望时，我便如闪耀的萤火似的，熠熠地向暗中飞去了。

当杜尔伽节①，邻家的孩子们来屋里游玩时，我便要融化在笛声里，整日价在你心头震荡。

亲爱的阿姨带了杜尔伽节礼物来，问道："我们的孩子在哪里，姊姊？"妈妈，你将要柔声地告诉她："他呀，他现在是在我的瞳仁里，他现在是在我的身体里，在我的灵魂里。"

————————

① 即印度十月间的"难近母祭日"。

THE RECALL

The night was dark when she went away, and they slept.

The night is dark now, and I call for her, "Come back, my darling; the world is asleep; and no one would know, if you come for a moment while stars are gazing at stars."

She went away when the trees were in bud and the spring was young.

Now the flowers are in high bloom and I call, "Come back, my darling. The children gather and scatter flowers in reckless sport. And if you come and take one little blossom no one will miss it."

Those that used to play are playing still, so spendthrift is life.

I listen to their chatter and call, "Come back, my darling, for mother's heart is full to the brim with love, and if you come to snatch only one little kiss from her no one will grudge it."

召唤

她走的时候，夜间黑漆漆的，他们都睡了。

现在，夜间也是黑漆漆的，我唤她道："回来，我的宝贝；世界都在沉睡；当星星互相凝视的时候，你来一会儿是没有人知道的。"

她走的时候，树木正在萌芽，春光刚刚来到。

现在花已盛开，我唤道："回来，我的宝贝。孩子们漫不经心地在游戏，把花聚在一块，又把它们散开。你如果走来，拿一朵小花去，没有人会发觉的。"

那些常常在游戏的人，仍然还在那里游戏，生命总是如此地浪费。

我静听他们的空谈，便唤道："回来，我的宝贝，妈妈的心里充满着爱，你如果走来，仅仅从她那里接一个小小的吻，没有人会妒忌的。"

THE FIRST JASMINES

Ah, these jasmines, these white jasmines!

I seem to remember the first day when I filled my hands with these jasmines, these white jasmines.

I have loved the sunlight, the sky and the green earth;

I have heard the liquid murmur of the river through the darkness of midnight;

Autumn sunsets have come to me at the bend of a road in the lonely waste, like a bride raising her veil to accept her lover.

Yet my memory is still sweet with the first white jasmines that I held in my hand when I was a child.

Many a glad day has come in my life, and I have laughed with merrymakers on festival nights.

On grey mornings of rain I have crooned many an idle song.

I have worn round my neck the evening wreath of bakulas woven by the hand of love.

Yet my heart is sweet with the memory of the first fresh jasmines that filled my hands when I was a child.

第一次的茉莉

呵，这些茉莉花，这些白的茉莉花！

我仿佛记得我第一次双手满捧着这些茉莉花，这些白的茉莉花的时候。

我喜爱那日光，那天空，那绿色的大地；

我听见那河水淙淙的流声，在漆黑的午夜里传过来；

秋天的夕阳，在荒原上大路转角处迎我，如新妇揭起她的面纱迎接她的爱人。

但我想起孩提时第一次捧在手里的白茉莉，心里充满着甜蜜的回忆。

我生平看过许多快活的日子。在节日宴会的晚上，我曾跟着说笑话的人大笑。

在灰暗的雨天的早晨，我吟哦过许多飘逸的诗篇。

我颈上戴过爱人手织的醉花的花圈，作为晚装。

但我想起孩提时第一次捧在手里的白茉莉，心里充满着甜蜜的回忆。

THE BANYAN TREE

O, you shaggy-headed banyan tree standing on the bank of the pond, have you forgotten the little child, like the birds that have nested in your branches and left you?

Do you not remember how he sat at the window and wondered at the tangle of your roots that plunged underground?

The women would come to fill their jars in the pond, and your huge black shadow would wriggle on the water like sleep struggling to wake up.

Sunlight danced on the ripples like restless tiny shuttles weaving golden tapestry.

Two ducks swam by the weedy margin above their shadows, and the child would sit still and think.

He longed to be the wind and blow through your rustling branches, to be your shadow and lengthen with the day on the water, to be a bird and perch on your topmost twig, and to float like those ducks among the weeds and shadows.

榕树

喂，你站在池边的蓬头榕树，你可曾忘记了那小小的孩子，就像那在你的枝上筑巢又离开了你的鸟儿似的孩子？

你不记得他怎样坐在窗内，诧异地望着你那深入地下的纠缠的树根么？

妇人们常到池边，汲了满罐的水去。你的大黑影便在水面上摇动，好像睡着的人挣扎着要醒来似的的。

日光在微波上跳舞，好像不停不息的小梭在织着金色的花毡。

两只鸭子挨着芦苇，在芦苇影子上游来游去，孩子静静地坐在那里想着。

他想做风，吹过你萧萧的枝杈；想做你的影子，在水面上，随了日光而俱长；想做一只鸟儿，栖息在你的最高枝上；还想做那两只鸭，在芦苇与阴影中间游来游去。

BENEDICTION

Bless this little heart, this white soul that has won the kiss of heaven for our earth.

He loves the light of the sun, he loves the sight of his mother's face.

He has not learned to despise the dust, and to hanker after gold.

Clasp him to your heart and bless him.

He has come into this land of an hundred cross-roads.

I know not how he chose you from the crowd, came to your door, and grasped your hand to ask his way.

He will follow you, laughing and talking and not a doubt in his heart.

Keep his trust, lead him straight and bless him.

Lay your hand on his head, and pray that though the waves underneath grow threatening, yet the breath from above may come and fill his sails and waft him to the haven of peace.

Forget him not in your hurry, let him come to your heart and bless him.

祝福

祝福这个小心灵，这个洁白的灵魂，他为我们的大地，赢得了天的接吻。

他爱日光，他爱见他妈妈的脸。

他没有学会厌恶尘土而渴求黄金。

紧紧把他抱在你心里，并且祝福他。

他已来到这个歧路百出的大地上了。

我不知道他怎么要从群众中选出你来，来到你的门前，抓住你的手问路。

他笑着，谈着，跟着你走，心里没有一点儿疑惑。

不要辜负他的信任，引导他到正路，并且祝福他。

把你的手按在他的头上，祈求着：底下的波涛虽然险恶，然而从上面来的风会鼓起他的船帆，送他到和平的港口的。

不要在忙碌中把他忘了，让他来到你的心里，并且祝福他。

THE GIFT

⁓ↄ℮ↄ⁓

I want to give you something, my child, for we are drifting in the stream of the world.

Our lives will be carried apart, and our love forgotten.

But I am not so foolish as to hope that I could buy your heart with my gifts.

Young is your life, your path long, and you drink the love we bring you at one draught and turn and run away from us.

You have your play and your playmates. What harm is there if you have no time or thought for us?

We, indeed, have leisure enough in old age to count the days that are past, to cherish in our hearts what our hands have lost for ever.

The river runs swift with a song, breaking through all barriers. But the mountain stays and remembers, and follows her with his love.

赠品

　　我要送些东西给你，我的孩子，因为我们同是漂泊在世界的溪流中的。

　　我们的生命将被分开，我们的爱也将被忘记。

　　但我却没有那样傻，希望能用我的赠品来买你的心。

　　你的生命正是青青，你的道路也长着呢，你一口气饮尽了我们带给你的爱，便回身离开我们跑了。

　　你有你的游戏，有你的游伴。如果你没有时间同我们在一起，如果你想不到我们，那有什么害处呢？

　　我们呢，自然地，在老年时，会有许多闲暇的时间，去计算那过去的日子，把我们手里永久丢失了的东西，在心里爱抚着。

　　河流唱着歌很快地游去，冲破所有的堤防。但是山峰却留在那里，忆念着，满怀依依之情。

MY SONG

This song of mine will wind its music around you, my child, like the fond arms of love.

This song of mine will touch your forehead like a kiss of blessing.

When you are alone it will sit by your side and whisper in your ear, when you are in the crowd it will fence you about with aloofness.

My song will be like a pair of wings to your dreams, it will transport your heart to the verge of the unknown.

It will be like the faithful star overhead when dark night is over your road.

My song will sit in the pupils of your eyes, and will carry your sight into the heart of things.

And when my voice is silent in death, my song will speak in your living heart.

我的歌

我的孩子，我这一支歌将用它的乐声围绕你，好像那爱情的热恋的手臂一样。

我这一支歌将触着你的前额，好像那祝福的接吻一样。

当你只是一个人的时候，它将坐在你的身旁，在你耳边微语着；当你在人群中的时候，它将围住你，使你超然物外。

我的歌将成为你的梦的翼翅，它将把你的心移送到不可知的岸边。

当黑夜覆盖在你路上的时候，它又将成为那照临在你头上的忠实的星光。

我的歌又将坐在你眼睛的瞳仁里，将你的视线带入万物的心里。

当我的声音因死亡而沉寂时，我的歌仍将在你活泼泼的心中唱着。

THE CHILD-ANGEL

They clamour and fight, they doubt and despair, they know no end to their wranglings.

Let your life come amongst them like a flame of light, my child, unflickering and pure, and delight them into silence.

They are cruel in their greed and their envy, their words are like hidden knives thirsting for blood.

Go and stand amidst their scowling hearts, my child, and let your gentle eyes fall upon them like the forgiving peace of the evening over the strife of the day.

Let them see your face, my child, and thus know the meaning of all things; let them love you and thus love each other.

Come and take your seat in the bosom of the limitless, my child. At sunrise open and raise your heart like a blossoming flower, and at sunset bend your head and in silence complete the worship of the day.

孩子天使

他们喧哗争斗，他们怀疑失望，他们辩论而没有结果。

我的孩子，让你的生命到他们当中去，如一线镇定而纯洁之光，使他们愉悦而沉默。

他们的贪心和妒忌是残忍的；他们的话，好像暗藏的刀刃，渴欲饮血。

我的孩子，去，去站在他们愤懑的心中，把你的和善的眼光落在他们上面，好像那傍晚的宽宏大量的和平，覆盖着日间的骚扰一样。

我的孩子，让他们望着你的脸，因此能够知道一切事物的意义；让他们爱你，因此使他们也能相爱。

来，坐在无垠的胸膛上，我的孩子。在朝阳出来时，开放而且抬起你的心，像一朵盛开的花；在夕阳落下时，低下你的头，默默地做完这一天的礼拜。

THE LAST BARGAIN

"Come and hire me," I cried, while in the morning I was walking on the stonepaved road.

Sword in hand, the King came in his chariot.

He held my hand and said, "I will hire you with my power."

But his power counted for nought, and he went away in his chariot.

In the heat of the midday the houses stood with shut doors.

I wandered along the crooked lane.

An old man came out with his bag of gold.

He pondered and said, "I will hire you with my money."

He weighed his coin one by one, but I turned away.

It was evening. The garden hedge was all aflower.

The fair maid came out and said, "I will hire you with a smile."

Her smile paled and melted into tears, and she went back alone into the dark.

The sun glistened on the sand, and the sea waves broke waywardly.

A child sat playing with shells.

He raised his head and seemed to know me, and said, "I hire you with nothing."

From thenceforward that bargain struck in child's play made me a free man.

最后的买卖

早晨，我在石铺的路上走时，我叫道："谁来雇用我呀。"

皇帝坐着马车，手里拿着剑走来。

他拉着我的手，说道："我要用权力来雇用你。"

但是他的权力算不了什么，他坐着马车走了。

正午炎热的时候，家家户户的门都闭着。

我沿着屈曲的小巷走去。

一个老人带着一袋金钱走出来。

他斟酌了一下，说道："我要用金钱来雇用你。"

他一个一个地数着他的钱，但我却转身离去了。

黄昏了。花园的篱上满开着花。

美人走出来，说道："我要用微笑来雇用你。"

她的微笑黯淡了，化成泪容了，她孤寂地回身走进黑暗里去。

太阳照耀在沙地上，海波任性地浪花四溅。

一个小孩坐在那里玩贝壳。

他抬起头来，好像认识我似的，说道："我雇你不用什么东西。"

在这个小孩的游戏中做成的买卖，使我从此以后成了一个自由的人。

附录

泰戈尔传 (郑振铎)

他的诗正如这个天真烂漫的天使
的脸;看着他,就知道一切事物的意义,
就感到和平,感到安慰,并且知道真
正相爱。

一

　　许多批评家都说，诗人是"人类的儿童"。因为他们都是天真的，和善的。在现在的许多诗人中，罗宾德拉纳特·泰戈尔（Rabindranath Tagore）更是一个"孩子的天使"。他的诗正如这个天真烂漫的天使的脸；看着他，就知道一切事物的意义，就感到和平，感到安慰，并且知道真正相爱。著《泰戈尔的哲学》的 S. Radhakrishnan 说：泰戈尔著作之流行，之所以能引起全世界人的兴趣，一半在于他思想中的高超的理想主义，一半在于他作品中的文学的庄严与美丽。他的著作在现今尤有特殊的价值；因为这个文明世界自经大战后，已宣告物质主义的破产了。（参阅《泰戈尔的哲学》第二页）

二

　　泰戈尔是彭加尔（Bengal）[①] 地方的人。

　　印度是一个"诗之国"，诗就是印度人日常生活的一部分。新生的儿童来到这个世界上所受的一次祝福，就是用韵文唱的。孩子大了，如做了不好的事，他母亲必定背诵一首小诗告诉他这种行为的不对。在初等学校里，教了字母之后，学生所上的第一课书就是一首诗。许多青年的心里所受的最初的教训就是："两个伟大的祝福，能

[①] 即孟加拉。——编者注

消除这个艰苦的世界的恐怖的，就是尝诗的甘露与交好的朋友。"许多印度人写的书，也都是用诗的形式来写的；文法的条规，数学的法则，乃至博物学、医学、天文学、化学、物理学，都是如此。结婚的时候，唱的是欢愉之诗；死尸火葬的时候，他们对于死人的最后的说话，也是引用印度的诗篇。

在这个"诗之国"里，产生了这个伟大的诗人泰戈尔自然是没有什么奇怪的。

三

泰戈尔的生辰是一八六一年五月七日。他的家庭是印度的望族，他的长辈出了许多名人，他的同辈和晚辈也出了好些哲学家、艺术家。他自己曾说道："我小的时候所得的大利益，就是文学与艺术的空气弥漫于我们家里。"他的接待室里，每天晚上灯都亮着，客人来往不绝。他的兄弟 Ganendra 在家里搭起戏台，演过 Pandit Taskaratna 做的戏；他的侄子 Jyotiprokash 也教过他作诗。他的父亲 Dabendranath Tagore 更是当时的一个天才。泰戈尔在此优越的环境中成长，他的伟大的诗才受了不少的灌溉，自然是要出芽、生枝，而且开花、结果。

泰戈尔的母亲死的很早。他在儿童时代，寂寞而不快乐，很少出外——到街上，或园林里——去游玩。离了家塾以后，他进了本地的东方学校，师范学校，又进了英国人办的彭加尔学校，又被送到英国去学法律。但是对学校里的刻板而无味的生活，他十分憎恶。无论到哪个学校，都不过一年就退学回家。他父亲很知道他的性情，并不强迫他去服从学校里的残酷而不明了儿童个性的教师，只在家里请了人教他。

但他还有两个大教师呢！一个是自然界，一个是平民。泰戈尔他自己告诉过我们：自然界就是他的亲爱的同伴；她手里藏了许多东西，要他去猜。泰戈尔的猜法真是奇怪！凡是她给他猜的东西，他没有不一猜就中的。这因为他与自然界相处已久而且很深了，他很小的时候就爱她。他家里有一棵榕树，他少时常到树下洗澡游玩，到了后来，还记得它：

绕缠的树根从你枝干上悬下，呵，古老的榕树呀，你日夜不动地站着，好像一个苦行的人在那里忏悔，你还记住那个孩子，他的幻想曾同你的影子一同游戏的吗？

以后，刚格（Ganges）河①的风光，喜马拉亚山的景色，几乎无不深深地印在他明彻的心镜里。

他与他父亲的工人交际得很密切。他在 Sal aidah 地方管理他父亲的农产时，除了帕德马河，他的最好的朋友就是一般农民了。所以他竟成了他们内在的精神的表现者。

在泰戈尔二十三岁的时候，他与一个女子结了婚。这个婚姻是理想的快乐的结合。到后来小孩们降临他家的时候，他又得了新的教师了。《新月集》就是在那时写的。在世界文学家里，没有一本诗集比他这个《新月集》描写儿童更好而且更美丽、真切的了。母亲的永久

① 即恒河。——编者注

的神秘与美，与孩子之天真，都幽婉地温和地达出了十二分。且看：

大家都知道你是十分喜欢甜的东西的，——这就是他们所以叫你贪嘴么？

嘻！那么，他们把我们喜欢你的人叫做什么呢？

这句母亲对她孩子说的话是如何诙谐而慈爱呀！总之，天真烂漫的儿童世界，教导他以不少的真理。在他三十五岁前后，他的夫人死了。他的爱女、他的爱儿也都相继而夭亡。这个可怕的阴忧笼罩在他身上，使他做出世界上最柔和甜美的情歌，使他的灵魂更有力，更尖锐。他的诗，在这个时期所写的也很优美。后来遂转其笔锋去做颂神之歌，不复作情诗。

这蔓延的痛苦，因爱与欲望更深邃而成为人类家庭里的悲哀与快乐，这就是永远融合、流溢在我诗人心中发出来的歌声中的东西了。

这是他《颂神诗集》[①]（Gitanjali）中的一句，我们读了觉得他还有余痛浮绕在笔端呢。

一九〇二年，他创办了一个"和平之院"——山铁尼克当（Shantiniketan）学校——校址在 Bolpus 离加尔各答不远。在那个地方，他的两个大师——自然界与儿童——已融合在一起了，这个学校的教法，用印度的古法，而参以西方的方法，是一种森林学校。凡是到那里参观过的人，都以为泰戈尔的计划非常成功。以前只有二三个学生，现在[②]已经增加到二百人。他得的诺贝尔文学奖金，已捐

---

① 即《吉檀迦利》。——编者注

② 这里系指作者撰写此文的时代，即 20 世纪 20 年代。——编者注

入此校为基金。听说，他的著作所得的利益也都消耗在这个学校里。
Macdonald 君做了一篇关于这个"和平之院"的游记，说："无论什么
东西在那个地方都是和平、自然而且快活。"任何好争斗、好烦恼的
成人，一到了这个"和平之院"，听见早晨的儿童的清脆抑扬的歌声，
没有不忘记他的困恼的生之担负的！

　　他的著作多自己译成英文。最初出版的是《园丁集》。此诗集一
出，凡是说英语的民族与懂得英语的民族，无不大为惊讶。以前泰戈
尔的名字，除印度外，知道的人极少。自此以后，这个白衣的和平天
使的威力立刻弥漫于全人类之间，瑞典的文学会，也立刻把一九一三
年的诺贝尔文学奖金，致之于他的座前。

　　一九一五年，他到了日本，受日人极狂热的欢迎。一九二〇年，
他到了美国，这个拜金国的国民也是非常鼓舞地去迎接他。一九二一
年，他到了德国。德国受欧战之刺激，思想大变，对于这个东方的
"自然之子"，更表示一种特别的敬意。据柏林通信说，他讲演的地
方，德人特别布成森林的景色，因为大家都知道，泰戈尔不仅是"人
类的儿童"，而且是"自然的儿童"。

　　在一九一九年，法郎士、巴比塞、罗素、爱伦开诸人，在法国
巴黎发起了一个"光明团"，提倡永久和平的、非战的运动，泰戈尔
也在里边。他又尽力鼓吹印度的独立，曾向英国政府请愿许印度的自
治，他们竟因此把他的"勋爵"（Sir）头衔取消。

四

泰戈尔的文学运动，开始得极早。在他十四岁的时候，即已开始做剧本。十九岁时，他做了第一篇小说，因此著名。后来继续做了不少的剧本，当时即已在彭加尔及加尔各答各剧场演出。到了现在，加尔各答还在那里演唱他的戏。

他的著作，初时只传布在家庭内，后来才刊登于 Cyanankur 月刊上。他们同他定约，做诗的投稿者。他的散文著作，最初也登载在这个杂志上。

他的著作，最初都是用彭加尔文写的；凡是说彭加尔话的地方，没有人不日日歌诵他的诗歌。后来由他自己及他的朋友将许多种诗陆续译成英文，诗集有《园丁集》《新月集》《采果集》《飞鸟集》《吉檀迦利》《爱者之贻与歧路》；剧本有：《牺牲及其他》《邮局》《暗室之王》《春之循环》；论文集有《生之实现》《人格》《国家主义》；杂著有《我的回忆》《饿死及其他》《家庭与世界》等。

在彭加尔文里，据印度人说，他的诗较英文写的尤为美丽。一个印度人对 W. B. Yeats 说："我每天读泰戈尔，读他一行，可以把世上一切的烦恼都忘了。"他自己也说：

我的歌坐在你的瞳人里。将你的视线，带入万物的心里。

我的歌声，虽因死而沉寂；但是我的诗歌，仍将从你的活着的心里唱出来。

是的，泰戈尔的歌声虽有时沉寂，但是只要有人类在世上，他的微妙幽婉之诗，仍将永远由生人的心中唱出来的。

他的戏剧和小说，与诗也有同样的感化力。一个印度的批评家说："他的英雄与女英雄都是出于平常人之中的，他们的淳朴的快乐与忧愁，泰戈尔用异常的内在的沉刻的情绪，用音乐似的词句，写出来给我们看。"

就是他的论文，也是充溢着诗的趣味与音乐似的词句。他总之是一个诗人。

五

"他是我们圣人中的第一个人：不拒绝生命，而能说出生命之本身的，这就是我们所以爱他的原因了。"

这是一个印度人的话。但我们的意见也是如此：

我们所以爱他，就是因为他是不拒绝生命，而能说出生命之本身的。

本文的参考书：

（1）K. Roy: R. Tagore: The Man and His Poetry.

（2）R. Tagore: My Reminiscences.

（3）C. Martin: Poets of the Democracy.

（4）W. B. Yeats: Introduction to "Gitanjali".

（5）"Crescent Moon" and Other Poeme, by R. Tagore.

附录

泰戈尔来华（徐志摩）

绕缠的树根从你枝干上悬下，呵，古老的榕树呀，你日夜不动地站着，好像一个苦行的人在那里忏悔，你还记住那个孩子，他的幻想曾同你的影子一同游戏的吗？

　　泰戈尔在中国，不仅已得普遍的知名，竟是受普遍的景仰。

　　问他爱念谁的英文诗，十余岁的小学生，就自信不疑地答说泰戈尔。在新诗界中，除了几位最有名神形毕肖的泰戈尔的私淑弟子以外，十首作品里至少有八九首是受他直接或间接的影响的。这是可惊的状况，一个外国的诗人，能有这样普及的引力。

　　现在他快到中国来了，在他青年的崇拜者听了，不消说，当然是最可喜的消息，他们不仅天天竖耳企踵地在盼望，就是他们梦里的颜色，我猜想，也一定多增了几分妩媚。现世界是个堕落沉寂的世界；我们往常要求一二伟大圣洁的人格，给我们精神的慰安时，每每不得已上溯已往的历史，与神化的学士艺才，结想象的因缘，哲士、诗人与艺术家，代表一民族一时代特具的天才；可怜华族，千年来只在精神穷窭中度活，真生命只是个追忆不全的梦境，真人格亦只似昏夜池水里的花草映影，在有无虚实之间，谁不想念春秋战国才智之盛，谁不永慕屈子之悲歌，司马之大声，李白之仙音；谁不长念应生之逍遥，东坡之风流，渊明之冲淡？我每想及过去的光荣，不禁疑问现时人荒心死的现象，莫非是噩梦的虚景，否则何以我们民族的灵海中，曾经有过偌大的潮迹，如令何至于沉寂如此？孔陵前子贡手植的楷树，圣庙中孔子手植的桧树，如其传话是可信的，过了二千几百年，经了几度的灾劫，到现在还不时有新校从旧根上生发；我们华族天才的活力，难道还不如此桧此楷？

　　什么是自由？自由是不绝的心灵活动之表现。斯拉夫民族自开国起直至十九世纪中期，只是个庞大暗哑的无光的空气中苟活的怪物，但近六七十年来天才累出，突发大声，不但惊醒了自身，并且惊醒了所有迷梦的邻居。斯拉夫伟奥可怖的灵魂之发现，是百年来人类史上最伟大的一件事迹。华族往往以睡狮自比，这又泄漏我们想象力之堕落；期望一民族回复或取得吃人噬兽的暴力者，只是最下流"富国强兵教"的信徒，我们希望以后文化的意义与人类的目的明定以后，这类的谬冤可以渐渐的销匿。

精神的自由，决不有待于政治或经济或社会制度之妥协，我们且看印度。印度不是我们所谓已亡之国吗？我们常以印度、朝鲜、波兰并称，以为亡国的前例。我敢说我们见了印度人，不是发心怜悯，是意存鄙蔑（我想印度是最受一班人误解的民族，虽同在亚洲大部分人以为印度人与马路上的红头阿三是一样同样的东西！）就政治看来，说我们比他们比较地有自由，这话勉强还可以说。但要论精神的自由，我们只似从前的俄国，是个庞大暗哑在无光的气圈中苟活的怪物，他们（印度）却有心灵活动的成绩，证明他们表面政治的奴缚非但不曾压倒，而且激动了他们潜伏的天才。在这时期他们连出了一个宗教性质的政治领袖——甘地——一个实行的托尔斯泰；两个大诗人，伽利达撒（Kalidasa）与泰戈尔。单是甘地与泰戈尔的名字，就是印度民族不死的铁证。

东方人能以人格与作为，取得普通的崇拜与荣名者，不出在"国富兵强"的日本，不出在政权独立的中国，而出于亡国民族之印度——这不是应发人猛省的事实吗？

泰戈尔在世界文学中，究占如何位置，我们此时还不能定，他的诗是否可算独立的贡献，他的思想是否可以代表印族复兴之潜流，他的哲学（如其他有哲学）是否有独到的境界——这些问题，我们没有回答的能力。但有一事我们敢断言肯定的。就是他不朽的人格。他的诗歌，他的思想，他的一切，都有遭遗忘与失时之可能，但他一生热奋的生涯所养成的人格，却是我们不易磨羁的纪念。[泰戈尔生平的经过，我总觉得非是东方的，也许印度原不能算东方（陈寅恪君在海外常常大放厥词，辩印度之为非东方的。）] 所以他这回来华，我个人最大的盼望，不在他更推广他诗艺的影响，不在传说他宗教的哲学的乃至于玄学的思想，而在他可爱的人格，给我们见得到他的青年，一个伟大深人的神感。他一生所走的路，正是我们现代努力于文艺的青年不可免的方向。他一生只是个不断的热烈的努力，向内开豁他天赋的才智，自然吸收应有的营养。

他境遇虽则一流顺利，但物质生活的平易，并不反射他精神生活之不艰险。我们知道诗人、艺术家的生活，集中在外人捉摸不到的内心境界。历史上也许有大名人一生不受物质的苦难，但决没有不经心灵界的狂风暴雨与沉郁黑暗时期者。葛德① 是一生不愁衣食的显例，但他在七十六岁那年对他的友人说他一生不曾有过四星期的幸福，一生只是在烦恼痛苦劳力中。泰戈尔是东方的一个显例，他的伤痕也都在奥秘的灵府中的。

我们所以加倍地欢迎泰戈尔来华，因为他那高超和谐的人格，可以给我们不可计量的慰安，可以开发我们原来淤塞的心灵泉源，可以指示我们努力的方向与标准。可以纠正现代狂放恣纵的反常行为，可以摩掌我们想见古人的忧心，可以消平我们过渡时期张皇的意义，可

---

① 即歌德。

以使我们扩大同情与爱心，可以引导我们入完全的梦境。

如其一时期的问题，可以综合成一个现代的问题，就只是"怎样做一个人？"泰戈尔在与我们所处相仿的境地中，已经很高尚地解决了他个人的问题，所以他是我们的导师、榜样。

他是个诗人，尤其是一个男子，一个纯粹的入他最伟大的作品就是他的人格。这话是极普通的话，我所以要在此重复地说，为的是怕误解。人不怕受人崇拜，但最怕受误解的崇拜。葛德说，最使人难受的是无意识的崇拜。泰戈尔自己也常说及。他最初最后只是个诗人一艺术家如其你愿意一他即使有宗教的或哲理的思想，也只是他诗心偶然的流露，决不为哲学家谈哲学，或为宗教而训宗教的。有人喜欢拿他的思想比这个那个西洋的哲学，以为他是表现东方一部的时代精神与西方合流的；或是研究他究竟有几分的耶稣教几分是印度教一这类的比较学也许在性质偏爱的人觉得有意思，但于泰戈尔之为泰戈尔，是绝对无所发明的。譬如有人见了他在山氏尼开顿（Santiniketan）学校里所用的晨祷：

Thou art our Father. Do you help us to know thee as Father. We bow down to Thee. Do thou never afflict us, Father, by causing a separation between Thee and us. O thou selfrevealing one, O Thou Parent of the universe, purge away the multitude of our sins, and send unto us whatever is good and noble, to Thee, from whom spring joy and goodness nay, who art all goodness thyself, to Thee we bow down now and for ever.

耶教人见了这段祷告一定拉本家，说泰戈尔准是皈依基督的，但回头又听见他们的晚祷：

The Deity who is in fire and water, nay, who pervades the Universe through, and through, and makes His abode in tiny plants and towering forests—to such a Deity we bow down for ever and ever.

这不最明显的泛神论吗？这里也许有 Lucretius 也许有 Spinoza 也许有 Upanishads[①] 但决不是天父云云的一神教，谁都看得出来。回头在揭檀迎利[②] 的诗里，又发现什么 Lia 既不是耶教的，又不是泛神论。结果把一般专好拿封条拿题签来支配一切的，绝对的糊涂住了，他们一看这事不易办，就说泰戈尔是诗人，不是宗教家。也不是专门的哲学家。管他神是一个或是两个或是无数或是没有，诗人的标准，只是诗的境界之真；在一般人看来是不相容纳的冲突（因为他们只见字面），他看来只是一体的谐合（因为他能超文字而悟实在）。

同样的在哲理方面，也就有人分别研究，说他的人格论是近于讹的，说他的艺术论是受讹影响的……这也是劳而无功的。

自从有了大学教授以来，尤其是美国的教授，学生忙的是：比较哲学，比较宪法学，比较人种学，比较宗教学，比较教育学，比较这样，比较那样，结果他们意想把最高粹的思想艺术，也用比较的方法来研究——我看倒不如来一门比较大学教授学还有趣些！

思想之不是糟粕，艺术之不是凡品，就在他们本身有完全、独立、纯粹不可分析的性质。类不同便没有可比较性，拿西洋现成的宗

---

① Lucretius: 卢克莱修；Spinoza: 斯宾诺莎；Upanishads:《奥义书》。

② 即《吉檀迦利》。

教哲学的派别去比凑一个创造的艺术家，犹之拿唐采芝或王玉峰去比附真纯创造的音乐家一样的可笑，一样的隔着靴子搔痒。

我们只要能够体会泰戈尔诗化的人格，与领略他充满人格的诗文，已经尽够的了，此外的事自有专门的书呆子去顾管，不劳我们费心。

我乘便又想起一件事，一九一三年泰戈尔被选得诺贝尔奖金的电报到印度时，印度人听了立即发疯一般的狂喜，满街上小孩大人一齐呼庆祝，但诗人在家里，非但不乐，而且叹道："我从此没有安闲日子过了！"接着下年英政府又封他为爵士，从此，真的，他不曾有过安闲时日。他的山氏尼开顿竟变了朝拜的中心，他出游欧美时，到处受无上的欢迎，瑞典、丹麦几处学生，好像都为他举行火把会与提灯会，在德国听他讲演的往往累万，美国招待他的盛况，恐怕不在英国皇太子之一下。但这是诗人所心愿的幸福吗，固然我不敢说诗人便能完全免除虚荣心，但这类群众的哄动，大部分只是葛德所谓无意识的崇拜，真诗人决不会艳羡的，最可厌是西洋一般社交太太们，她们的宗教照例是英雄崇拜；英雄愈新奇，她们愈乐意，泰戈尔那样的道貌岸然，宽袍布帽，当然加倍地搔痒了她们的好奇心，大家要来禾口这远东的诗圣，握握手，亲热亲热，说几句照例的肉麻话……这是近代享盛名的一点小报应，我想性爱恬淡的泰戈尔先生，临到这种情形，真也是说不出的苦。据他的英友恩厚之告诉我们说他近来愈发厌烦嘈杂了，又且他身体也不十分能耐劳，但他就使不愿意，却也很少显示于外，所以他这次来华，虽则不至受社交太太们之窘，但我们有机会瞻仰他言论丰采的人，应该格外地体谅他，谈论时不过分去劳乏他，演讲能节省处节省，使

他下口我们能如家人一般地相与，能如在家乡一般地舒服，那才对
得他高年跋涉的一番至意。

七月六日

（原刊 1923 年 9 月 10 日《小说月报》第 14 卷第 9 号）

附录

徐志摩 1924 年 5 月 12 日 在北京真光剧场的演讲

我的歌坐在你的瞳人里。将你的视线，
带入万物的心里。
我的歌声，虽因死而沉寂；但是我的
诗歌，仍将从你的活着的心里唱出来。

　　我有几句话想趁这个机会对诸君讲，不知道你们有没有耐心听。泰戈尔先生快走了，在几天内他就离别北京，在一两个星期内他就告辞中国。他这一去大约是不会再来的了。也许他永远不能再到中国。

　　他是六七十岁的老人，他非但身体不强健，他并且是有病的。所以他要到中国来，不但他的家属，他的亲戚朋友，他的医生，都不愿意他冒险，就是他欧洲的朋友，比如法国的罗曼·罗兰，也都有信去劝阻他。他自己也曾经踌躇了好久，他心里常常盘算他如其到中国来，他究竟能不能够给我们好处，他想中国人自有他们的诗人、思想家、教育家，他们有他们的智慧、天才、心智的财富与营养，他们更用不着外来的补助与载刺，我只是一个诗人，我没有宗教家的福音，没有哲学家的理论，更没有科学家实利的效用，或是工程师建设的才能，他们要我去做什么，我自己又为什么要去，我有什么礼物带去满足他们的盼望。他真的很觉得迟疑，所以他延迟了他的行期。但是他也对我们说到冬天完了春风吹动的时候（印度的春风比我们的吹得早），他不由得感觉了一种内迫的冲动，他面对着逐渐滋长的青草与鲜花，不由得抛弃了，忘却了他应尽的职务，不由得解放了他的歌唱的本能，和着新来的鸣雀，在柔软的南风中开怀的讴吟。同时他收到我们催请的信，我们青年盼望他的诚意与热心，唤起了老人的勇气。他立即定夺了他东来的决心。他说趁我暮年的肢体不曾僵透，趁我衰老的心灵还能感受，决不可错过这最后唯一的机会，这博大、从容、礼让的民族，我幼年时便发心朝拜，与其将来在黄昏寂静的境界中萎衰的惆怅，毋宁利用这夕阳未暝的光芒，了却我晋香人的心愿？

他所以决意地东来，他不顾亲友的劝阻，医生的警告，不顾自身的高年与病体，他也撇开了在本国一切的任务，跋涉了万里的海程，他来到了中国。

自从四月十二日在上海登岸以来，可怜老人不曾有过一半天完整的休息，旅行的劳顿不必说，单就公开的演讲以及较小集会时的谈话，至少也有了三四十次！他的，我们知道，不是教授们的讲义，不是教士们的讲道，他的心府不是堆积货品的栈房，他的辞令不是教科书的喇叭。他是灵活的泉水，一颗颗颤动的圆珠从他心里兢兢地泛登水面都是生命的精液；他是瀑布的吼声，在白云间，青林中，石罅里，不住地欢响；他是百灵的歌声，他的欢欣、愤慨、响亮的谐音，弥漫在无际的晴空。但是他是倦了。终夜的狂歌已经耗尽了子规的精力，东方的曙色亦照出他点点的心血染红了蔷薇枝上的白露。

老人是疲乏了。这几天他睡眠也不得安宁，他已经透支了他有限的精力。他差不多是靠散拿吐瑾① 过日的。他不由得不感觉风尘的厌倦，他时常想念他少年时在恒河边沿拍浮的清福，他想望椰树的清荫与曼果的甜瓢。

但他还不仅是身体的疲劳，他也感觉心境的不舒畅。这是很不幸的。我们做主人的只是深深地负歉。他这次来华，不为游历，不为政治，更不为私人的利益，他熬着高年，冒着病体，抛弃自身的事业，备尝行旅的辛苦，他究竟为的是什么？他为的只是一点看不见的情感，说远一点，他的使命是在修补中国与印度两民族间中断

---

① 散拿吐瑾，一种药物。

千余年的桥梁。说近一点，他只想感召我们青年真挚的同情。因为他是信仰生命的，他是尊崇青年的，他是歌颂青春与清晨的，他永远指点着前途的光明。悲悯是当初释迦牟尼证果的动机，悲悯也是泰戈尔先生不辞艰苦的动机。现代的文明只是骇人的浪费，贪淫与残暴，自私与自大，相猜与相忌，飓风似的倾覆了人道的平衡，产生了巨大的毁灭。芜秽的心田里只是误解的蔓草，毒害同情的种子，更没有收成的希冀。在这个荒惨的境地里，难得有少数的丈夫，不怕阻难，不自馁怯，肩上抗着铲除误解的大锄，口袋里满装着新鲜人道的种子，不问天时是阴是雨是晴，不问是早晨是黄昏是黑夜，他只是努力地工作，清理一方泥土，施殖一方生命，同时口唱着嘹亮的新歌，鼓舞在黑暗中将次透露的萌芽。泰戈尔先生就是这少数中的一个。他是来广布同情的，他是来消除成见的。我们亲眼见过他慈祥的阳春似的表情，亲耳听过他从心灵底里迸裂出的大声，我想只要我们的良心不曾受恶毒的烟煤熏黑，或是被恶浊的偏见污抹，谁不曾感觉他至诚的力量，魔术似的，为我们生命的前途开辟了一个神奇的境界，燃点了理想的光明？所以我们也懂得他的深刻的懊怅与失望，如其他知道部分的青年不但不能容纳他的灵感，并且存心的诬毁他的热忱。我们固然奖励思想的独立，但我们决不敢附和误解的自由。他生平最满意的成绩就在他永远能得青年的同情，不论在德国，在丹麦，在美国，在日本，青年永远是他最忠心的朋友。他也曾经遭受种种的误解与攻击，政府的猜疑与报纸的诬捏与守旧派的讥评，不论如何的谬妄与剧烈，从不曾扰动他优容的大量，他的希望，他的信仰，他的爱心，他的至诚，完全的托付青年。我的须，我的发是白的，但我的心却永远是青的，他常常的对我们说，只要青年是我的知己，我理想的将来就有着落，我乐观的明灯永远不致暗淡。他不能相信纯洁的青年也会坠落在怀疑、猜忌、卑琐的泥潭，他更不能相信中国的青年也会沾染不幸的污点。他真不预备在中国遭受意外的待遇。他很不自在，他很感觉异样的怆心。

因此精神的懊丧更加重他躯体的倦劳。他差不多是病了。我们当然很焦急地期望他的健康，但他再没有心境继续他的讲演。我们恐怕今天就是他在北京公开讲演最后的一个机会。他有休养的必要。我们也绝不忍再使他耗费有限的精力。他不久又有长途的跋涉，他不能不有三四天完全的养息。所以从今天起，所有已经约定的集会，公开与私人的，一概撤销，他今天就出城去静养。

我们关切他的一定可以原谅，就是一小部分不愿意他来做客的诸君也可以自喜战略的成功。他是病了，他在北京不再开口了，他快走了，他从此不再来了。但是同学们，我们也得平心地想想，老人到底有什么罪，他有什么负心，他有什么不可容赦的犯案？公道是死了吗？为什么听不见你的声音？

他们说他是守旧，说他是顽固。我们能相信吗？他们说他是"太迟"，说他是"不合时宜"，我们能相信吗？他自己是不能信，真的不能信。他说这一定是滑稽家的反调。他一生所遭逢的批评只是太新，太早，太急进，太激烈，太革命的，太理想的，他六十年的生涯只是不断的奋斗与冲锋，他现在还只是冲锋与奋斗。但是他们说他是守旧、太迟、太老。他顽固奋斗的对象只是暴烈主义、资本主义、帝国主义、武力主义、杀灭性灵的物质主义；他主张的只是创造的生活，心灵的自由，国际的和平，教育的改造，普爱的实现。但他说他是帝国政策的间谍，资本主义的助力，亡国奴族的流民，提倡裹脚的狂人！肮脏是在我们的政客与暴徒的心里，与我们的诗人又有什么关系？昏乱是在我们冒名的学者与文人的脑里，与我们的诗人又有什么亲属？我们何妨说太阳是黑的，我们何妨说苍蝇是真理？同学们，听信我的话，像他的这样伟大的声音我们也许一辈子再不会听着的了。留神目前的机会，预防将来的惆怅！他的人格我们只能到历史上去搜寻比拟。他的博大的温柔的灵魂我敢说永远是人类记忆里的一次灵绩。他的无边的想象是辽阔的同情使我们想起惠德曼[①]；他的博爱的福音与宣传的热心使我们记起托尔斯泰；他的坚韧的意志与艺术的天才使我们想起造摩西[②]像的密仡郎其罗[③]；他的诙谐与智慧使我们想象当年的苏格拉底与老聃！他的人格的和谐与优美使我们想念暮年的葛德[④]；他的慈祥的纯爱的抚摩，他的为人道不厌的努力，他的磅礴的大声，有时竟使我们唤起救主的心像，他的光彩，他的音乐，他的雄伟，使我们想念奥林必克[⑤]山顶的大神。他是不可侵凌的，不可逾越的，他是自然界的一个神秘的现象。他是三春和暖的南风，惊醒树枝上的新芽，增添处女颊上的红晕。他是普照的阳光。他是一派浩瀚的大水，从来不可追寻的渊源，在大地的怀抱中终古地流着，不息地流

---

① 惠德曼，通译惠特曼（1819—1892），美国诗人，著有《草叶集》等。

② 摩西，《圣经》故事中古代犹太人的领袖。

③ 密仡郎其罗，通译米盖朗琪罗（1475—1564），意大利文艺复兴时期的雕塑家、画家。

④ 葛德，通译歌德（1749—1832），德国诗人。

⑤ 奥林必克，通译奥林匹斯，希腊东北部的一座高山，古代希腊人视为神山，希腊神话中的诸神都住在山顶。

着，我们只是两岸的居民，凭借这慈恩的天赋，灌溉我们的田稻，苏解我们的消渴，洗净我们的污垢。他是喜马拉雅积雪的山峰，一般的崇高，一般的纯洁，一般的壮丽，一般的高傲，只有无限的青天枕藉他银白的头颅。

人格是一个不可错误的实在，荒歉是一件大事，但我们是饿惯了的，只认鸠形与鹄面是人生本来的面目，永远忘却了真健康的颜色与彩泽。标准的低降是一种可耻的堕落：我们只是踞坐的井底青蛙，但我们更没有怀疑的余地。我们也许端详东方的初白，却不能非议中天的太阳。我们也许见惯了阴霾的天时，不耐这热烈的光焰，消散天空的云雾，暴露地面的荒芜，但同时在我们心灵的深处，我们岂不也感觉一个新鲜的影响，催促我们生命的跳动，唤醒潜在的想望，仿佛是武士望见了前峰烽烟的信号，更不踌躇地奋勇前向？只有接近了这样超轶的纯粹的丈夫，这样不可错误的实在，我们方始相形的自愧我们的口不够阔大，我们的嗓音不够响亮，我们的呼吸不够深长，我们的信仰不够坚定，我们的理想不够莹澈，我们的自由不够磅礴，我们的语言不够明白，我们的情感不够热烈，我们的努力不够勇猛，我们的资本不够充实……

我自信我不是恣滥不切事理的崇拜，我如其曾经应用浓烈的文字，这是因为我不能自制我浓烈的感想。但是我最急切要声明的是，我们的诗人，虽则常常招受神秘的徽号，在事实上却是最清明，最有趣，最诙谐，最不神秘的生灵。他是最通达人情，最近人情的。我盼望有机会追写他日常的生活与谈话。如其我是犯嫌疑的，如其我也是性近神秘的（有好多朋友这么说），你们还有适之①先生的见证，他也说他是最可爱最可亲的一个人：我们可以相信适之先生绝对没有"性近神秘"的嫌疑！所以无论他怎样的伟大与深厚，我们的诗人还只是有骨有血的人，不是野人，也不是天神。唯其是人，尤其是最富情感的人，所以他到处要求人道的温暖与安慰，他尤其要我们中国青年的同情与情爱。他已经为我们尽了责任，我们不应，更不忍辜负他的期望。同学们！爱你的爱，崇拜你的崇拜，是人情不是罪孽，是勇敢不是懦怯！

附录

郑振铎译泰戈尔诗拾遗

现在少年的光阴过去了，我的生命如同一个果子一般，没有什么东西耗费了，只等着完完全全地带着她的充实甜美的负担，贡献她自己。

采果集

2

我少年时候的生命如同一朵花一般——当春天的微飔来乞求于她的门上时，一朵花从她的丰富里失去一两瓣花片也并不觉得损失。

现在少年的光阴过去了，我的生命如同一个果子一般，没有什么东西耗费了，只等着完完全全地带着她的充实甜美的负担，贡献她自己。

4

我醒过来，于晨光中找到他的信。

我不知道它里面说的是什么，因为我不会读它。

让那聪明人一个人读他的书吧，我不去惊扰他。因为谁知道他能不能读信中所说的话呢？

让我把它擎在我的前额，把它印在我的心里。

当夜天渐渐的静默了，群星一个一个出来的时候，我要把它展开，摆在我膝上，静悄悄地坐着。

沙沙的林叶要高声对我读它，潺潺的溪流要曼吟它，七颗聪明的星也要从天上对我歌唱它。

我不能找到我所要找的，我不能知道我所学的；但是，这封不能读的信却减轻了我的担负，却使我的思想转而为歌。

15

你的话是简单的，我的主人，但却不是谈论你的那些人的话。

我懂得你的群星的语言，懂得你的树林的静默。

我知道我的心开放起来如一朵花；我知道我的生命自己充满着，如一条伏泉。

你的歌，如同从寂寞的雪地飞来的鸟一般，飞来在我的心里筑巢。在四月温热的时候，我满足地等待这个快乐季候的来临。

23

诗人的心于风与水的声音中间，在生命之波上浮游而且跳舞。

现在太阳西下了，黑暗的天空降落在海面，如垂下的睫毛落在倦眼上一样。这是他把笔搁下，在这沉默的永久秘密当中，使他的思想沉入深渊之底的时候了。

24

夜间黑漆漆的，你的微睡深沉在我身的安慰里。

醒吧，喂，爱情的痛苦，因为我不知道怎样去开那扇门，我只好站在门外。

时间等着，群星守着，风静止着，沉默很沉重地压在我心里。

醒吧，爱情，醒吧！倒满我的空杯，用歌的呼吸激扰夜间吧。

25

晨雀唱着歌。

在晨光未露之前，在如毒龙之夜还把天空握在他的冷黑圈子里的时候，他什么时候有早晨的语言呢？

告诉我，晨雀呀，由天与树叶盖成的两重夜里，东方的使者他怎么会找到他的路来到你的梦中？

当你叫道"太阳正在走来，夜要过去了"时，世界是不会相信你的。

喂，睡着的人，醒醒吧！

显露你的前额，等着光的第一次祝福，在快乐的忠实里，与晨雀一块唱歌吧。

爱者之贻

4

她接近我的心，如草花之接近土地；她对于我之甜蜜，如睡眠之于疲倦的肢体。我对于她的爱情是我充溢的生命的流泛，如河水之秋涨，寂静地迅速流逝着。我的歌与我的爱情是一体，如溪流的潺湲，以他金色波涛的水流歌唱着。

5

如果我占有了天空和他所有的星星，占有了地球和他无穷的宝藏，我仍是要求增加的。但是，如果她成了我的，则我虽仅有这个世界上的最小一隅，即已感到很满足了。

9

妇人，你的篮子很重，你的肢体也疲倦了。你要走多远的路？你所求的是什么呢？道路很长，太阳下的尘土太热了。

看，湖水深而且满，水色黑如乌鸦的眼睛。湖岸倾斜而衬着绿草。

把你的倦足伸到水里去。午潮的风，把他的手指穿过你的头发；鸽子咕咕地唱他的睡歌，树叶微语着那安眠于绿荫中的秘密。

时间逝了，太阳落了，有什么要紧？横过荒地的道路在朦胧中失去了，又有什么要紧？

23

我爱这沙岸。这里有寂静的池沼，鸭子在那里呷呷地叫着，龟伏在日光底下曝着；黄昏时，有些飘游的渔舟，藏在茂草中间。

你爱那有树的对岸。那里，阴影聚在竹丛的枝上；妇人们捧了水瓶，从弯曲的小巷里出来。

同是这一条河在我们中间流着。它对它两岸唱的是同样的歌。我在星光底下，一个人躺在沙上，静听着水声；你也在早晨的光明里，坐在斜坡的边上，静听着。然而，我从它那里听得的话你却不知道，而它向你说的密语，对于我也永远是一个秘密。

25

　　我握住你的双手，我的心跃入你眼的黑睛里，寻求你这永远避我而逃出于言语之外者。

　　然而我知道我必须满足我的变动与易灭的爱情。因为我们有一回曾在街道中遇见。我有力量带你通过这个众多世界的群众，经过这个歧路百出的旅程么？我有食粮能供给你经过架着死亡之桥的黑暗的空罅么？

28

　　我梦见她坐在我头的旁边，手指温柔地撩动我的头发，奏着她的接触的和谐。我望着她的脸，晶莹的眼泪颤动着，直到不能说话的痛苦烧去我的睡眠，如一个水泡似的。

　　我坐了起来，看见窗外银河的光辉，如一个着火的沉默的世界。我不知道她在这个时候，有没有和我做着同韵律的梦。

29

我想，当我们的眼光在篱间相遇时，我有些话要对她说。但她走过去了。而我对她说的话，却如一只小艇，日夜在时间的每一个波浪上冲摇着。它似乎在秋云上行驶着，在不住地探问着；又似乎变成黄昏的花朵盛开着，在落照中寻求它已失的时间。我对她说的话，又如萤火似的，在我心上闪熠着，于失望的尘中，寻觅它的意义。

30

春花开放出来，如不言之爱的热烈的苦痛。我旧时歌声的回忆，随了他们的呼吸而俱来。我的心突然长出欲望的绿叶来。我的爱没有来，但她的接触是在我的肢体上，她的语声也横过芬芳的田野而到来。她的眼波在天空的忧愁的深处；但是她的眼睛在哪里呢？她的吻香飞熠在空气之中，但是她的樱唇在哪里呢？

36

我的镣铐，你在我心上奏着乐。我和你整日地游戏着，我把你当成我的装饰品。我们是最好的朋友，我的镣铐。有些时候我惧怕你，但我的惧怕使我爱你更甚。你是我漫漫黑夜的伴侣，我的镣铐。在我和你说再会之前，我向你鞠躬。

38

我飘浮在上面的川流，当我少年时，它迅速而湍急地流着。春风微微地吹拂着，林花盛放如着火；鸟儿们不停息地歌唱着。

我旋晕地急驶着，被热情的水流所带走。我没有时间去看，去感觉，去把全世界拿到我身边来。

现在，那个少年是消失了。我登到岸上来，我能够听见万物的深沉的乐音，天空也对我展开了它缀满繁星的心。

42

你不过是一幅图画而不是如那些明星一样的真实，如这个灰尘一样的真实么？它们都随着万物的脉息而搏动着，但你则完全固定着你的静止的画成的形象。

你以前曾和我一同走着，你的呼吸温暖，你的肢体吟唱着生命之歌。我的世界，在你的语声里找到它的话语，用你的容光来接触我的心。你突然地停步不进了，伫立在永久的荫旁，剩我一人向前走去。

生命如一个小孩，它笑着，一边跑着，一边喋喋地谈着死：它招呼我向前走去，我跟随着那不可见的脚步；但你立在那里，停在那些灰尘与明星之外，你不过是一幅图画。

不，那是不能够的。如果生命之流在你那里停止了，那么它便也要停止滚滚的河流，便也要停止具有色彩绚烂的足音的黎明的足迹了。如果你的头发的闪熠的微光在无望的黑暗中暝灭了，那么夏天的绿荫也将和她的梦境一同死去了。

我忘了你，这会是真的么？我们匆匆地、头也不回地走着。忘了路旁篱落上开着的花。在忘掉一切的情景中，它们的香气不知不觉进入我们的呼吸，还充满着乐音。你已离开了我的世界，而去坐在我的生命的根上，所以这便是遗忘——回忆迷失在它自己的深处。

你已不再在我的歌声之前了，但你现在与他们是一个。你偕了晨光的第一条光线而到我这里来。到了夕阳的最后的金光消失时，我才不见了你。就是这时以后，我也仍在黑暗中寻求你。不，你不仅仅是一幅图画。

44

当你死的时候，你对于我以外的一切，算是死了，你算是从世界的万物里消失不见了。但却完全地重生在我的忧愁里。我觉得我的生命完成了，男人与女人对于我永远成了一体。

45

携了美丽与秩序到我的艰苦的生命里来吧，妇人，当你生时，你曾携过他们到我的屋里。请扫除掉时间的尘屑，倒满了空的水瓶，备补了所有的疏忽。然后请打开神庙的内门，点燃明烛，让我们在我们的上神之前沉默地相遇着。

48

我每天走着那条旧路。我携果子到市集里去，我牵我的牛到草地上去，我划我的船渡过那条河水，所有这些路，我都十分熟悉。

有一天清晨，我的篮子里满装了东西。许多人在田野里忙着，牧场上停息着许多牛；地球的胸因喜米谷的成熟而扬起着。

大气中突然起了一阵颤动，天空似乎和我的前额接吻。我的心警醒起来，如清晨之跳出雾中。

我忘记了循原路走去。我离开原路走了几步，我看着我的熟悉的世界，而觉得奇异，好像一朵花，我以前所见的仅是它的蓓蕾。

我日常的智慧害了羞。我在这万物的仙国里飘游着。我那天清晨的失路，寻到我的永久的童年，可算是我生平最好的幸运。

50

"来，月亮，下来吻我爱的前额。"母亲这样说着，她把她的小女孩抱在膝上。那时，月亮如梦似的微笑着。夏天的微香在黑暗中偷偷地进来；夜鸟的歌声也从杧果林的阴影密蔽的寂静里送过来。在一个远处的村间，从一个农夫的笛里，吹来一阵悲哀音调的泉源。年轻的母亲坐在土阶上，孩子在她的膝上，她温柔地咿唔道："来，月亮，下来吻我爱的前额。"她有时抬头看天上的光明，有时又低首看在她臂间的地上的光明。我诧异着月亮的恬静。

孩子笑着，学着她母亲的话："来，月亮，下来。"母亲微笑着，明月照澈的夜也微笑着。我，做诗的人，这孩子的母亲的丈夫，隐在看不见的地方，凝视着这幅图画。

51

　　早秋的时节天上没有一片云。河水溢到岸沿来，冲刷着立在浅水边的倾侧的树的裸根。长而狭的路，如乡村的渴舌，没入河水中去。

　　我的心满盈盈的，我朝四周观望着，看着沉默的天空，流泛的河水，觉着快乐正在外面展延着，真朴如儿童脸上的微笑。

57

　　这个秋天是我的，因为她在我心头震撼着。她的闪耀的足铃在我的血管里丁零地响着，她的雾色的面纱，扰动着我的呼吸。我在所有我的梦中知道她的棕色头发的接触。她走出去，在颤抖的树叶上，那些树叶在我的生命的脉搏里跳舞；她的两眼从青的天空上微笑着，从我那里饮啜他们的光明。

歧路

12

我的心呀，紧紧地握住你的忠诚，天要黎明了。

"允诺"的种子已经深深地埋在土里，不久便要发芽了。

睡眠如一颗蓓蕾，将要向光开放它的心，沉静也将找到它的声音。

你的担负要变成你的赠赐，你的痛苦也将烛照你的道路，这日子
是近了。

16

你黎明时走到我的门口，唱着歌；我被你从睡梦中惊醒。我很生
气，你便悄悄地走开了。

你正午时走进门来，向我要水喝；我正在做事，我很恼怒，你便
遭到斥责地走出去了。

你黄昏时，带了熊熊的火炬走进来。

我看你好像是一个恐怖者，我便把门关上了。

现在，在夜半的时候，我孤寂地坐在黑漆漆的房里，却要叫被我斥走的你回来了。

20

天色晦暝，雨淅沥地下着。

愤怒的电光从破碎的云幕里射下来。

森林如一只囚在笼中的狮子，失望地摇着鬃毛。

在这样的一天，在狂风呼呼地扑打他们的翼膀的中间，让我在你面前找到我的平安吧。

因为这忧郁的天空，已荫盖着我的孤独，使你与我的心的接触的意义更为深沉。

77

"旅客，你到什么地方去？"

"我沿着林阴的路，在红色的黎明中，到海里沐浴去。"

"旅客，那个海在什么地方？"

"它在这个河的尽处,在黎明开朗为清晨的地方,在白昼没落为黄昏的地方。"

"旅客,同你一块儿来的有多少人?"

"我不知道怎样去数他们。

"他们提着点亮了的灯,终夜在旅行着;他们经过陆与水,终日在歌唱着。"

"旅客,那个海有多远?"

"它有多远,正是我们所要问的。

"它的波涛的澎湃,涨泛到天上,当我们静止不言之时。它永远地似乎在近,却又在远。"

"旅客,日光是灼场的热。"

"是的,我们的旅路是长而艰难的。

"谁精神疲倦了便歌唱,谁心里懦怯了便歌唱。"

"旅客,如果黑夜包围了他们呢?"

"我们便将躺下去睡,直睡到新的清晨偕了它的歌声而照耀着,及海的呼唤在空中浮泛着时。"

世纪末日

1

这个世纪的最后的太阳，在西方的血红的云与嫉忌的旋风中落下去了。

各个国家的自私的赤裸裸的热情，沉醉于贪望之中，跟了钢铁的相触声与复仇的咆哮的歌声而跳舞着。

2

饥饿的国家，它自己会在自己的无耻的供养里暴烈地愤怒地烧灼起来。

因为它已把世界当做它的食物而舐着嚼着，一口气吞了下去。

它膨胀了，又膨胀了。

甚至在它的非圣洁的宴会中，天上突然落下武器，贯穿了它的粗大的心胸。

3

地平线上所现的红色的光，不是和平的曙光，我的祖国呀。

它是火葬的柴火的光，把那伟大的尸体——国家的自私的心——烧成了灰的，它已因自己的嗜欲过度而死去了。

你的清晨则正在东方的忍耐的黑暗之后等待着。乳白而且静寂。

4

留意着呀，印度。

带了你的信仰的祭礼给那个神圣的朝阳。让欢迎它的第一首颂歌在你的口里唱出。

"来吧，和平，你上帝自己的大痛苦的女儿。"

"带了你的惬意的宝藏，强毅的利剑。"

"与你的冠于前额的温和而来吧。"

5

不要羞馁，我的兄弟们呀，披着朴素的白袍，站在骄傲与威权之前。

让你的冠冕是谦虚的，你的自由是灵魂的自由。

天天建筑上帝的座位在你的贫穷的广漠的赤地上，而且要知道庞巨的东西并不是伟大的，骄傲的东西并不是永久的。

爱者之贻

　　我的歌呀，你的市场在什么地方呢？夏天的微风里杂着学者鼻烟的气味；人们不休地辩论那"油依赖着桶或是桶依赖着油"的问题；黄色的稿子对于逝水似的无价值的人生蹙着眉峰；你的市场是在这些地方么？我的歌叫道：唉，不是，不是。

　　我的歌呀，你的市场在什么地方呢？幸福的人住在云石的宫殿里，十分骄傲，十分肥胖。他的书放在架上，皮装金字，且有奴仆为之拂去尘埃，他们的洁白的纸上写着的是奉献于冥冥之神的；你的市场是在这个地方么？我的歌喘着气答道：不是，不是。

　　我的歌呀，你的市场在什么地方呢？青年学生，坐在那里，头低到书上，他的心飘荡在青年的梦境里；散文在书桌上巡掠着，诗歌则深藏在心里。你的市场是在这个地方么？你愿意在那种尘埃满布的无秩序中捉迷藏么？我的歌迟疑不决地沉静着。

　　我的歌呀，你的市场在什么地方呢？新妇在家里忙碌着，当她一得闲暇，便跑到卧室里去，急急地从她枕下取出一本小说，这书被婴儿粗忽地玩弄着，而且充满着她的头发香。你的市场是在这个地方么？我的歌叹息一声颤震着，意思未定。

　　我的歌呀，你的市场在什么地方呢？禽鸟的歌声，宏纤毕闻；溪流的潺湲，也能清晰地听到，世界的一切琴弦将他们的音乐倾注在两个翱翔的心上。你的市场是在这个地方么？我的歌突然地叫道：是的，是的。

昨夜我在花园里，献我的青春的白沫腾跳的酒给你。你举杯在唇边，开了两眼微笑着；而我掀起你的面纱，解开你的辫发，让你的沉默而甜柔的脸贴在我的胸前，明月的梦正泛溢在微睡的世界里。

今天在清露冷凝的黎明的静谧里，你走向大神的寺院去，沐过浴，穿着白色长袍，手里拿着满篮鲜花。我在这黎明的静谧里，在到寺院去的寂寞的路旁的树荫下面，头低垂着。

无题

静听，我的心。他的笛声，就是野花的气息的音乐，闪亮的树叶、光耀的流水的音乐，影子回响着蜜蜂之翼的音乐。

笛声从我朋友的唇上，偷走了微笑，把这微笑蔓延在我的生命上。

花环

我的花如乳、如蜜、如酒，我用一条金带把他们结成了一个花环。但他们逃避了我的注意，飞散开了，只有带子留着。

我的歌声如乳、如蜜、如酒，他们存在于我跳动的心的韵律里。但他们，这暇时的爱者，又展开翼膀，飞了开去，我的心在沉寂中跳动着。

我所爱的美人，如乳、如蜜、如酒，她的唇如早晨的玫瑰；她的眼如蜂一般的黑。我使我的心静静的，只怕惊动了她。但她却也如我的花、我的歌一样，逃避了我，只有我的爱情留着。

有许多次，春天在我们的房外敲着门，那时，我忙着做我的工，你也不曾答理他。现在，只有我一个人在那里，心里病着，而春天又来了，但我不知道怎样才能叫他从门口回转身去。当他走来而欲以快乐的冠给我戴时，我们的门是闭着的，现在他来时所带的是忧愁的赠品，我却不能不开门让他走进来了。

（以上译诗原载 20 世纪 20 年代出版的
《小说月报》和《文学周报》）

《爱的教育》
湖南文艺出版社
ISBN：978-7-5404-4684-0/开本：32开/定价：25.00元

意大利政府官方授权名家权威版本 意大利原版完整插图
荣获意大利驻华使馆颁发的"意大利政府文化奖"
世界儿童文学最高奖——国际安徒生奖所在"国际少年儿童读物联盟"（IBBY）推荐"青少年必读书目"之一
中华人民共和国教育部指定"中小学语文新课标课外阅读书目"之一
联合国教科文组织推荐《世界各国青少年必读系列丛书》

《假如给我三天光明》
湖南文艺出版社
开本：32开/定价：25.00元

人类意志力最伟大的代表典范作品
一本向光明、智慧、希望、仁爱引航的人生手册
世界文学史上无与伦比的杰作

《再别康桥·人间四月天》
湖南文艺出版社
开本：32开/定价：25.00元

新月派代表诗人&民国第一才女 诗歌精选合集
穿越半个多世纪的心灵交会 值得一生珍藏的绝美诗篇

《城南旧事》
湖南文艺出版社
ISBN：978-7-80220-805-6/开本：32开/定价：25.00元

林海音作品权威完整版
国家教育部推荐读物，入选"二十世纪中文小说一百强"
五十年来最让人温暖的感动